TV's
Most Wanted

Selected titles in Brassey's *Most Wanted* Series

TV's
Most Wanted

The Top 10 Book of Crazy Casting, Off-Camera Clashes, and Other Oddities

Douglas Tonks

Brassey's, Inc.

WASHINGTON, D.C.

Library of Congress Cataloging-in-Publication Data

Tonks, Douglas.
TV's most wanted : the top 10 book of crazy casting,
off-camera clashes, and other oddities / Douglas
Tonks.—1st ed.
p.   cm.
Includes bibliographical references and index.
ISBN 1-57488-515-4 (pbk. : alk. paper)
1. Television programs—United
States—Miscellanea.   2. Television
broadcasting—United
States—Anecdotes.   I. Title.

PN1992.9 .T66   2003
791.45'75'0973—dc21
2002038480

Printed in Canada on acid-free
paper that meets the American National Standards
Institute Z39-48 Standard.

Brassey's, Inc.
22841 Quicksilver Drive
Dulles, Virginia 20166

First Edition

10 9 8 7 6 5 4 3 2 1

Contents

Photographs

Acknowledgments

While researching and writing a book, especially one as heavy in facts as this one, an author becomes indebted to a number of people along the way. I would like to thank Stu Shea for his help in getting this project started and for advice throughout. Frank Peppiatt, Ron Tonks, and Sheldon Chad offered helpful suggestions; and Scott Barnard, Jim Barnard, Ken Tonks, and Bob Barnard provided comment on the manuscript, for which I am grateful. I also appreciate the help of Sandy Stert Benjamin and Howard Benjamin of The Interview Factory; Barry Adelman, Stephanie Fry, and Jeff James of Dick Clark Productions; and Jack Bowman, Julie Burnett, Nancy Davis, Charlene Epple, Marcia Minor, Donald Stephens,

Doug Thompson, and George Yanok for their assistance in finding and obtaining photographs. Finally, I thank my wife, Francesca Peppiatt, specifically for her help and support with this book and more generally for everything else.

Introduction

There is a television set in almost every living room in the United States. Wherever we turn we see something relating to television or TV shows. It's gotten so we can't escape the influence of television, and we have a hard time imagining what our lives would be like without it. We easily forget that TV has not been around that long.

Commercial television did not take its first tentative steps until the late 1930s. Development was hampered somewhat by World War II, and as late as 1946 most cities had only one television station, if they had any at all. The number of TV sets in the country could be counted in the thousands. Early networks consisted of only a handful of stations. NBC initially had two stations, one in New York City and one in Schenectady, New York, the home of General Electric's broadcasting labs. They later added Philadelphia to become, with all of three stations, the largest network of the time. The DuMont network had stations in New York and Washington (even though the number of TV sets in the nation's capital likely didn't extend into three figures). The signal from eastern networks didn't work its way to Chicago and the Midwest until 1949.

Things have certainly changed in just over fifty years—we are now faced with an explosion of stations available through cable. *TV's Most Wanted* revels in the TV culture that has developed during that time. Readers might expect a book of TV lists to include the longest-running show (*Meet the Press* has been on the air since 1947) or the highest-rated show (the final episode of *M*A*S*H,* "Goodbye, Farewell, and Amen," attracted well over 100 million viewers), but that information is fairly easy to come by. Instead, *TV's Most Wanted* celebrates television's more unusual side. There's a list of celebrated actors who appeared as Special Guest Villains on *Batman.* Another list explores visitors to *Gilligan's Island,* who seemingly could come and go as they pleased while Gilligan, the Skipper, and the other castaways were stranded for more than a decade. Whose names have appeared in the most titles of

TV shows? That answer is here. Are there any animals that starred in their own shows? Lassie and Flipper might quickly come to mind, but we list eight others as well. There is also a list of TV series that were taken off the air most quickly, which includes such clunkers as *Turn-On,* a comic travesty from 1969 that guest star Tim Conway insists was canceled before its first episode even finished airing.

TV's Most Wanted goes behind the scenes as well. Find out what Mickey Rooney thought about the character of Archie Bunker, or why Bing Crosby turned down the chance to play Lieutenant Columbo. Discover the TV past of Haley Joel Osment, who costarred in three different TV shows before finding success on the big screen. Learn about ten backstage feuds that made some of the most popular TV shows miserable places to work. Sit back and enjoy some of the most unusual TV lists ever compiled.

1
Connected by Television

Since the advent of television, some events have been so compelling that people have gathered around their TV sets to experience them together. Even though viewers were spread out across the country, the act of everyone watching the same thing at the same time made these communal events.

1. *SEE IT NOW*

The first time the entire nation simultaneously received a live commercial broadcast was on November 18, 1951. This program was *See It Now,* a public affairs series hosted by radio journalist Edward R. Murrow. That first broadcast was presented in split-screen live shots of the Brooklyn Bridge and the Golden Gate Bridge. Murrow pointed out that this was the first time that anyone could look at both the East Coast and the West Coast at the same moment.

2. THE KENNEDY ASSASSINATION

The nation clustered around TV screens when the news of the assassination of John F. Kennedy broke. Two days after the murder on November 22, 1963, accused assassin Lee Harvey Oswald was being transferred from the Dallas, Texas, city jail to the county jail. The transfer was broadcast live, so when Jack Ruby shot Oswald, it was in plain sight of the viewing public. The day after that, Kennedy's funeral was held in Washington, D.C., and the nation caught a glimpse of John F. Kennedy Jr., on his third birthday, saluting his slain father for the final time.

3. THE BEATLES ON *THE ED SULLIVAN SHOW*

Breaking news is obviously something that television does well, but TV is also very effective in documenting cultural events whose significance is only recognized years later. One such event was the first appearance of the Beatles on *The Ed Sullivan Show*. The February 9, 1964, broadcast, the Beatle's first appearance on live U.S. television, was in all respects a sensation. Kids across the country demanded that their parents tune in the program, which resulted in the highest ratings any regularly scheduled show had ever received to that time. Although it certainly sparked a lot of excitement when it was broadcast, no one realized how the culture would change as a result of what they had seen.

4. THE FIRST MOON LANDING

One of the most amazing broadcasts of all time didn't even come from this planet. The first time human beings ever landed on the moon was broadcast live on July 20, 1969, to a waiting world below. As astronaut Michael Collins held the command capsule of Apollo 11 in orbit around the moon, Neil Armstrong and Edwin "Buzz" Aldrin approached the lunar surface in the lunar module, Eagle. After the Eagle had landed, Armstrong and Aldrin prepared to step out onto the moon as the world held its breath. On the second step, Armstrong tripped the switch to deploy and activate an attached television camera to send the image of his first step on the moon back to Earth. He insists that his words were "That's one small step for *a* man, one giant leap for mankind," but that somehow the *a* dropped out of the transmission.

5. THE WATERGATE HEARINGS

A small, seemingly insignificant break-in at the headquarters of the Democratic National Commit-

tee during the 1972 presidential campaign effectively brought down the presidency of Richard M.
Nixon two years later. Although the event received
little attention at the time and Nixon went on to
overwhelming reelection, details emerged about
administration attempts to cover up the crime.
The scandal was named after the hotel, apartment, and office complex where it took place, and
as it expanded, it took on more and more significance. The Senate stepped into the fray to investi-
gate, and its hearings, held between May 17 and
August 7, 1973, were televised. For most of that
time, the networks rotated coverage, but the public access to the hearings caused a sensation—it
was estimated that 85 percent of all U.S. house-
holds watched some of the coverage throughout
the summer.

6.   THE CHALLENGER EXPLOSION

After the Apollo missions to the moon ended, public interest in the NASA space program waned
somewhat. The space agency reignited interest
when the first American civilian, teacher Christa
McAuliffe from New Hampshire, was scheduled to
take part in a mission aboard the Challenger space
shuttle. The Challenger liftoff on January 28,
1986, was seen by millions, and the nation went
into shock when, a minute after the shuttle took

off, it exploded. For those who didn't see the moment live, it was repeated in newscasts for days. In the explosion itself there was a stray plume of smoke that shot away from the main explosion. As an indication of how TV has affected people's judgment in expecting a happy ending from our TV shows, many people theorized that this was an escape pod by which all the astronauts would survive. The real world doesn't always have happy endings, of course, and no such escape pod was found.

7. THE FALL OF THE BERLIN WALL

The Cold War between the United States and the Soviet Union defined American foreign policy after World War II, which encompassed the entire history of commercial television. In fact, TV had never known a world without an Iron Curtain. When communism began to lose its hold over Eastern Europe, the national governments fell quickly. The most significant visual symbol of the Iron Curtain was the wall that cut through Berlin, the former capital of Germany, separating East Berlin from West Berlin. In November 1989 East Germany lifted some of the travel restrictions that had kept East Germans within its borders and began to demolish parts of the wall for checkpoints. Once started, however, the demolition could not be stopped, as people on both sides of the wall started taking bits and pieces. Television cameras from around the world recorded the fall of the wall and the symbolic fall of communism.

8. **O.J.'S WHITE BRONCO**

One of the most surreal TV events occurred on the afternoon of June 17, 1994. Football star and sometime actor O.J. Simpson had been accused of brutally killing his wife and another man. He was scheduled to turn himself in to Los Angeles police, who closed the street in front of the police station for him. Los Angeles TV stations had their cameras trained there in anticipation of the surrender, but after more than an hour of broadcasting a live shot of an empty street corner on almost every TV channel in town, the coverage moved inside the station as the police announced that Simpson had gone missing. A few hours later, his white Ford Bronco was spotted on a Southern California free-way, moving at about forty-five miles an hour. At this point the story went national, and the entire country watched the Bronco, accompanied by several police cars, slowly drive the empty free-way for several hours. Although virtually nothing was happening, the possibility of what *might* happen was horribly compelling, and most of the broadcast networks, as well as several cable chan-

nels, preempted their regular evening programming to show it. NBC even interrupted its coverage
of game five of the NBA finals between the New
York Knicks and the Houston Rockets to keep
viewers up to date. Tension was high as Simpson
returned to his house but wouldn't leave the
Bronco. There were reports that he had a gun, and
viewers wondered if they might see the former
sports hero commit suicide on the air. Simpson
was ultimately talked out of the car and taken into
custody to stand trial for the murders.

9. NEW YEAR'S EVE 1999

The turn of the millennium captured imaginations
around the world. This was the biggest New Year's
Eve in memory, and certainly the biggest potential
for international celebration television had ever
covered. Bringing the entire planet together in a
positive manner like few events had before, the
celebrations ringed the planet as the new millennium was ushered in from one time zone to the
next. Indelible images were transmitted from the
pyramids in Egypt (which were experiencing their
sixth new millennium), from the Eiffel Tower in
Paris, and from Times Square in New York. As
worries about computer failure and the "Y2K bug"
proved groundless, international celebrants were

free to look optimistically to the future, to the new century and millennium ahead.

10. **SEPTEMBER 11, 2001**

Some absolutely horrendous images were broadcast over live television during the terrorist attack on the World Trade Center in New York on September 11, 2001. Shortly before 9:00 on that Tuesday morning, a plane crashed into one of the twin towers. Details were sketchy in the moments following the disaster, but as soon as people heard the news, they raced to their televisions. There were no immediate pictures of the impact, but all cameras were trained on the towers for the aftermath. Just eighteen minutes later another jetliner flew into the second tower, this time on live TV for the world to see it as it happened. The significance of what had happened slowly became clear when a third airliner crashed into the Pentagon, the central headquarters of the American military in Washington, D.C. A fourth hijacked jetliner came down in rural Pennsylvania. Its passengers, learning of the attacks in New York and Washington, took control of the plane away from the hijackers, who were apparently targeting another Washington landmark. Television continued to broadcast as the twin towers collapsed, and viewers were left with images that would haunt them forever.

2
War Is Funny

It's a well-known saying that "War is hell," but in the hands of certain sitcom writers, war can be funny, too. World War II brought the reality of military life to a wide variety of the American public as people from all backgrounds and walks of life came together in the armed forces. Although there was certainly nothing funny about fighting the evils of Nazis and the other Axis powers, the common experience of life in the military shared by vast numbers of people made it an excellent subject for comedy. A number of situation comedies about war, some successful and some not so successful, have graced the television airwaves over the years.

1. *M*A*S*H*

On the short list for best television comedy of all time, *M*A*S*H* straddled the line between comedy and drama. At heart an antiwar comedy, *M*A*S*H* portrayed life in the 4077th Mobile Army Surgical Hospital and demonstrated the absurdist nature of keeping up morale and sanity at a time when life was both cheap and tenuous. *M*A*S*H* debuted in 1972, the tail end of the Vietnam War, and although it was set during the United Nations police action in Korea (which was never officially declared a war), it might as well have been in Vietnam. The comedy came from the idea that the doctors of the 4077th had to have a sense of humor about the conditions under which they were forced to perform surgery. Alan Alda starred as Captain "Hawkeye" Pierce (the character's real name was Benjamin Franklin Pierce), an irreverent doctor drafted into the army from his own practice in Maine. His first partner in crime was Captain Trapper John McIntyre, played by Wayne Rogers. They shared their quarters with Major Frank Burns (Larry Linville), a hypocritical by-the-book surgeon who, regardless of having a wife back in the States, carried on a hot-and-heavy affair with Major Margaret "Hot Lips" Houlihan (Loretta Swit). Despite this, Frank gave Pierce and McIntyre grief about the still they kept in the quarters and the endless parade of nurses coming in and out.

The ratings for *M*A*S*H* started out slow, but it became one of the most-watched shows on television throughout the seventies. Massive cast changes throughout its run seemed to have little effect on its popularity. By the time *M*A*S*H* aired its final episode on February 28, 1983, only Hawkeye, Hot Lips, and chaplain Father Francis Mulcahy (William Christopher) were left from the original cast. That two-and-a-half-hour special resulted in the largest audience ever for an episode of a TV series: a 60.3 rating, a 77 share (the percentage of all television sets currently in use tuned to that channel), and over 100 million viewers (estimates range from 103 million to 125 million).

2. *HOGAN'S HEROES*

Of all the wartime and military comedies, the series with the most questionable tastefulness must be *Hogan's Heroes,* which ran from 1965 until 1971. Behind the scenes of a Nazi prisoner-of-war camp seemed an unusual place to find humor. Yet *Hogan's Heroes* took that concept and, by making the Nazi captors bumbling rather than evil and making the Allied prisoners of Stalag 13 the real powers in control of the camp, brought about a very successful television show. Bob Crane, as

Colonel Robert Hogan, was the star of the show and the leader of the POWs. He and his men had tunnels under the barracks so they could come in and out of Stalag 13 on sabotage missions, full radio equipment to stay in contact with the rest of the Allied armed forces, and a fully functioning listening device in the camp commander's office.

The camp commander, Colonel Wilhelm Klink, was oblivious to the goings-on around him and instead spent his time trying to avoid a command on the Russian front. When Werner Klemperer agreed to play the part, he insisted that Colonel Klink never gain the upper hand in his dealings with Hogan. Klemperer was Jewish and had fled Nazi Germany as a child with his father, Otto Klemperer, conductor of the Berlin State Orchestra until 1933. Other actors who had run afoul of the Nazis were John Banner (camp guard Sergeant Schultz), a Viennese who was forced to flee his homeland, and Robert Clary (French POW Corporal Louis LeBeau), who was liberated from Buchenwald at the end of the war.

3. *THE PHIL SILVERS SHOW*

Originally titled *You'll Never Get Rich, The Phil Silvers Show* was also called *Sgt. Bilko* in reruns. Its original run was from 1955 to 1959. Phil Silvers

Photofest

From the time it went on the air in 1955, *The Phil Silvers Show* set
the standard for military sitcoms, and many imitators cropped up
over the years. In a typical scene, Silvers, as Sgt. Ernie Bilko, used
some fancy footwork to stay out of trouble.

played Master Sergeant Ernie Bilko, of course, in
what has become one of the most fondly remembered shows of its era. This show was not set in
wartime, so Bilko and his men were stationed in
fictional Fort Baxter, located in Kansas. Bilko always had some moneymaking scheme or another
cooking, and he was always one step ahead of the
camp's commanding officer, Colonel John Hall
(played by Paul Ford). Fast on his feet, Bilko also
had the ability to talk his way out of virtually any

situation. Of course, if the sergeant could act this way and get away with it, there was nothing to stop the rest of his platoon from trying the same thing. Sometimes it seemed that no one was in charge of Fort Baxter.

4. *F TROOP*

It's not just the modern military that can be funny, as *F Troop* so ably pointed out from 1965 until 1967. Set shortly after the Civil War on the western frontier, *F Troop* took its cue from *The Phil Silvers Show,* with Sergeant Morgan O'Rourke, played by Forrest Tucker, having the real power at Fort Courage. He and his subordinate Corporal Randolph Agarn, played by Larry Storch, had a secret deal with the local Native Americans to sell Native American souvenirs to any tourists who happened by. The commander of Fort Courage, Captain Wilton Parmenter, was oblivious to this entire setup. Portrayed by Ken Berry, Parmenter was an inept leader, who had only received his rank and post as a result of a mishap. As the opening theme song explained, Parmenter sneezed during a Civil War retreat, an action his fellow troops took as a signal to charge back into the skirmish, turning it into a Union victory. Parmenter became a hero and was awarded the Fort Courage command. The Native Americans who schemed with O'Rourke and Agarn

were Chief Wild Eagle (Frank DeKova) and Scream-
ing Chicken (Edward Everett Horton).

5. *McHALE'S navy*

Starring Ernest Borgnine as Lieutenant Commander Quinton McHale and airing from 1962 to
1966, *McHale's Navy* was essentially Bilko in the
navy. McHale commanded a PT boat in the Pacific
during World War II. McHale's crew, like Bilko's
platoon before them, were conniving, gambling
con artists. One familiar face was Gavin MacLeod
as Joseph "Happy" Haines. The commanding officer this time around was Captain Wallace Binghamton, portrayed by Joe Flynn, who was quite
entertaining in his frustration at his inability to
keep McHale and his men under control. Looking
for some help in that regard, Binghamton assigned
Ensign Charles Parker, played by Tim Conway, to
ride herd over the crew. While Parker was certainly
earnest enough in his attempts to do just that,
McHale always remained one step ahead of him,
keeping the brass guessing.

6. *ROLL OUT!*

Another World War II comedy, *Roll Out!* provided
viewers with something they hadn't seen before:
Most of the cast was made up of African Americans. The 5050th Quartermaster Trucking Com-

pany, also known as the "Red Ball Express," was a supply unit stationed in France, whose responsibility was to keep supplies flowing to the front line no matter what obstacles they may confront in that task. Once again the unruly unit paid little attention to actual military protocol, but they got the job done, and that was what mattered. The stars of *Roll Out!* were Stu Gilliam as Corporal "Sweet" Williams and Hilly Hicks as Private First Class Jed Brooks. Also appearing were a pre–*Saturday Night Live* Garrett Morris as Wheels, and Ed Begley Jr. as Lieutenant Robert Chapman. *Roll Out!* appeared Friday nights on CBS for three months at the end of 1973 and beginning of 1974.

7. *OPERATION PETTICOAT*

Back to the navy in the Pacific Theater during World War II, this series detailed the adventures of the *Sea Tiger,* a pink submarine (don't ask) that had to balance its regular sub crew along with a collection of young nurses. John Astin was Lieutenant Commander Matthew Sherman, and Richard Gilliland appeared as Lieutenant Nick Holden, the requisite Bilko character. The series was only a moderate success during the 1977–1978 season, so it was almost completely retooled for the next year. All but three of the original cast members were gone, including Astin, and a new crew that included Randolph Mantooth from *Emergency!* and Jo Ann Pflug took their place. The changes did nothing to help the ratings, and the new, improved crew disappeared after only four episodes. *Operation Petticoat* was an adaptation of a 1959 film that starred Cary Grant and Tony Curtis. As a side note, the original television cast included Tony's daughter, Jamie Lee Curtis, as one of the nurses.

8. *BROADSIDE*

As part of the war effort to get more men ready to fight in World War II, the navy started recruiting women in 1942 to take over secretarial and office work performed by men. These were Women Accepted for Volunteer Emergency Service, WAVES for short. *Broadside* was a one-season sitcom in 1964 and 1965. Also set in the Pacific during World War II, it portrayed a group of WAVES assigned to Ranakai Island, a base infested with sailors. That the WAVES created a turmoil was not unexpected, but it was quite vexing to the base's commanding officer, Commander Rogers Adrian. Played by Edward Andrews, he had become accustomed to his rather slow-moving and uneventful island (apparently Ranakai Island was a considerable distance from the enemy). Most of the time, Commander Adrian attempted to get the

WAVES transferred back to the mainland, but his efforts failed to bear fruit. Produced by the creator of *McHale's Navy, Broadside* has sometimes been considered a female version of that series.

9. *GOMER PYLE, U.S.M.C.*

A spin-off from *The Andy Griffith Show, Gomer Pyle, U.S.M.C.* followed Gomer, the Mayberry gas station attendant played by Jim Nabors, as he joined the marine corps at Camp Henderson, California. As established on *The Andy Griffith Show*, Gomer was naive and big-hearted but not very bright. His nemesis was his drill sergeant and platoon leader, Vince Carter (played by Frank Sutton), a loud-mouthed authoritarian who felt Gomer was trying to undermine him at every turn. For a few years Ronnie Schell appeared as another private, Duke Slater, this show's wannabe Bilko. Schell left the cast to star in his own sitcom (*Good Morning World,* which also happened to be Goldie Hawn's first regular TV series), but when that endeavor proved short-lived, he returned to the role of Slater, with that character promoted to be Sergeant Carter's new corporal.

Another member of Pyle's platoon was played by William Christopher, who went on to appear as Father Mulcahy in *M*A*S*H*. As an echo of the past, Camp Henderson's mess sergeant, Hacker, was played by Allan Melvin, who had previously appeared as one of Sergeant Bilko's primary henchmen on *The Phil Silvers Show*. Although *Gomer Pyle, U.S.M.C.* was on CBS from 1964 until 1970, the time of the primary American buildup in Vietnam, Private Pyle and Sergeant Carter somehow never faced the possibility of shipping overseas.

10. *C.P.O. SHARKEY*

Don Rickles starred as Chief Petty Officer Otto Sharkey, a drill instructor responsible for whipping his recruits, who came from a wide variety of social and ethnic backgrounds, into shape. A role like this couldn't have been more perfect for Rickles, who had already established a very successful career as an insult comic. Just as his comedy routine consisted of mocking and ridiculing others, so did his routine as a drill instructor. Sharkey was stationed at the Navy Training Center in San Diego, California.

Although Rickles couldn't have asked for a more appropriate setup, the television audience apparently was not terribly impressed. *C.P.O. Sharkey* came in at mid-season in 1976 but was not on NBC's schedule for 1977, and it might have been expected to go quietly off to sitcom limbo. But when the network was surprised by the quick cancellation of *The Sanford Arms*, its attempt to keep *Sanford and Son* going without either Sanford or his son, it was left with a hole in its Friday night schedule. *C.P.O. Sharkey* got the call to return, so like all good military men called to duty, it jumped to the task and ran for a second full year.

3
The Name in the Title

Most occupations have milestones that tell you when you've finally made it. For accountants, that might be making partner. For lawyers, arguing before the U.S. Supreme Court would be such a milestone. And for television performers, getting your name in the title is a sure way to demonstrate that you're someone to be contended with. And if you can achieve that more than once, that's just gravy. Here are some performers whose names have graced several titles.

1. DICK CLARK

The title for the man with his name in the most series' titles goes to Dick Clark. *The Dick Clark Show* (also known as *The Dick Clark Saturday Night Beechnut Show*), was a nighttime version of

American Bandstand, the weekday show that had made him famous. It ran for just over two years in the late fifties. Overlapping with it for a few months was *Dick Clark's World of Talent,* in which a celebrity panel reviewed aspiring (though usually professional) performers. More than a decade after *The Dick Clark Show,* his name returned to the title for *Dick Clark Presents the Rock and Roll Years,* a 1973–1974 nostalgic variety show. He tried his hand at a live variety show for a few months in 1978, *Dick Clark's Live Wednesday,* and then syndicated a late-night variety show in 1985–1986 to compete against *Saturday Night Live* called *Dick Clark's Nitetime.*

A successful producer as well as performer, Clark came to CBS's rescue in 1988 when, recovering from a writers' strike, the network needed to fill their schedule at the beginning of the season until their intended shows were ready. He jumped right in with another live variety hour, *Live! Dick Clark Presents.* But Clark never strayed far from nostalgia, and he remained on the air that year with the syndicated *Dick Clark's Golden Greats.*

Clark's name is on another show that, for obvious reasons, could never become a weekly series. Once every year Clark stands in New York's Times Square in the middle of the night to host *Dick Clark's New Year's Rockin' Eve.*

dick clark productions, inc.

Long a household name, Dick Clark came to prominence as host of *American Bandstand*. Clark hosted a number of series, including the annual *Dick Clark's New Year's Rockin' Eve* from New York City's Times Square.

2. **BILL COSBY**

Cosby is no slouch in the names department, either—he's lent his name to seven different programs (so far). The first and most obvious was *The Bill Cosby Show,* a 1969 sitcom in which he played Chet Kincaid, a phys ed teacher and coach. *The New Bill Cosby Show,* an hour-long variety series, followed in 1973. Cosby had also become involved in a Saturday morning cartoon, *Fat Albert and the Cosby Kids,* which ran on CBS from 1972 until 1984 (in 1979 it was renamed *The New Fat Albert Show* but remained essentially the same). Always interested in education, Cosby attempted with his next variety show to reach out primarily to children. Unfortunately, *Cos* lasted only a few weeks in 1976.

For the next few years, Cosby's primary television exposure was in Jell-O commercials, where he displayed an entertaining rapport with children. When he did return to evening series TV in 1984, he did so with a vengeance. Some critics were lamenting the death of the sitcom, but Cosby proved them wrong with *The Cosby Show,* in which he and Phylicia Ayers-Allen played Cliff and Clair Huxtable, a New York professional couple raising their five kids. (Phylicia Ayers-Allen later married sportscaster Ahmad Rashad and changed her name to Phylicia Rashad.)

Almost single-handedly Cosby revitalized the sitcom form. After an eight-year run, however, he was interested in something different and returned in 1994 with *The Cosby Mysteries,* playing retired detective Guy Hanks (borrowing his real-life wife's maiden name). The public wasn't used to seeing him in a serious role, and the program didn't last the year. In 1996 he returned to sitcoms as Hilton Lucas, a former airline employee downsized out of his job, with Phylicia Rashad returning as his wife, Ruth. This show was titled simply *Cosby.*

3.   LUCILLE BALL

Lucille Ball is likely the most recognized woman in television history. With husband Desi Arnaz, she essentially established the rules for sitcoms. Her first show, *I Love Lucy,* costarred Arnaz, and together they played Lucy and Ricky Ricardo. From the moment it premiered in 1951, *I Love Lucy* shot to the top of the ratings (it was usually the top series of the year and never dropped below number three) and stayed there for six years. It was so popular, in fact, that CBS scheduled reruns of *I Love Lucy* in its weeknight programming for another two years. At the end of the series in 1957, Ball and Arnaz tried something new: hour-long specials in which the Ricardos and their neighbors, the Mertzes, traveled to different locales. These specials were later collected as *The Lucy-Desi Comedy Hour.* Behind the scenes, unfortunately, the couple wasn't as happy as the TV characters, and the marriage dissolved.

Lucille Ball was a performer, of course, so in 1962 she returned in *The Lucy Show,* playing Lucy Carmichael, a widowed bank secretary. In the series' second year, Gale Gordon joined the cast as Lucy's boss and nemesis, Mr. Mooney. He would remain with Ball for the rest of her television career. Six years after *The Lucy Show* began, the program was changed to *Here's Lucy,* Lucy's last name was changed to Carter, and her real-life children, Desi Arnaz Jr. and Lucie Arnaz, were added to the cast. That show ran another six years. In 1986, twelve years after the end of *Here's Lucy,* Ball came back one more time in *Life with Lucy,* but the magic was gone and the show was canceled in less than two months.

4. BOB NEWHART

Bob Newhart has used just about every part of his name for a title of a TV show. His first series, 1961's *The Bob Newhart Show,* was a half-hour variety program. Although the show was wildly popular with critics and won an Emmy for Outstanding Achievement in the Field of Humor, it was not renewed after its first year. Newhart stayed away from another series for over ten years, but when he returned in 1972, this time with a sitcom also called *The Bob Newhart Show,* he was more successful. He played Chicago psychologist Bob Hartley, who interacted with a number of unusual patients in his practice. This program ran for six years, and when it finished Newhart didn't stay away for long.

In 1982, he was back as Dick Loudon, a Vermont innkeeper and writer. Since he had already used his full name for a title twice, he went with his last name, *Newhart,* for this show. It ran eight years, even longer than his previous series. And when *Newhart* finished, the comedian was back with another series in 1992, a scant two years later. But his full name had already been used in a title, as had his last name. The choice was obvious—the new show was titled *Bob* and featured Bob McKay, a greeting card and comic book artist. This series was not as successful, however, barely limping into its second season before being canceled in December 1993. But Newhart was back again in 1997 with *George & Leo,* playing George Stoody to Judd Hirsch's Leo Wagonman. The two characters were thrown together when George's son married Leo's daughter. Although it appeared that Newhart's use of different parts of his name in titles was over, that is not the case.

You guessed it—the comedian's full name is George Robert Newhart.

5. DINAH SHORE

Dinah Shore was the first woman to host a variety show, and each of her five programs included her name in the title. *The Dinah Shore Show* began in 1951 as a fifteen-minute musical program on Tuesdays and Thursdays before John Cameron Swayze's *Camel News Caravan,* where it ran for six years. Fifteen minutes didn't provide time for more than a couple of songs and maybe a short conversation with a guest, but it was enough to keep Shore's star bright.

In 1956 she hosted *The Dinah Shore Chevy Show,* monthly hour-long variety shows with the popular Chevrolet theme, "See the U.S.A. in your Chevrolet." The longer format allowed her to broaden her activities, providing room for large production numbers and sketch comedy with her guests. Shore took quickly to the new format, and the next year the show joined NBC's normal weekly schedule on Sunday evenings. In 1961 it dropped the sponsor's name and moved to Friday nights.

After her cancellation in 1963, Shore took a break from series television for a few years but returned to daytime TV in 1970, hosting *Dinah's*

Place, a half-hour talk show on NBC. She remained there for four years, but when *Dinah's
Place* was canceled in 1974, she jumped almost
immediately to a similar syndicated program expanded to ninety minutes. Titled simply *Dinah!,* it
ran for six years. But Shore was not completely
finished with evening television. She hosted one
final variety show, substituting for *The Carol Burnett Show* in the summer of 1976, called *Dinah
and Her New Best Friends,* which featured eight
up-and-coming performers.

6. DICK VAN DYKE

This tall, lanky actor became a TV icon as the star
of his own sitcom, *The Dick Van Dyke Show,* in
1961. As television writer Rob Petrie, Van Dyke
scored as a result of his likeability and comic ver-
satility. Although ratings were low at first and CBS
executives actually canceled it outright in 1962
before granting it a reprieve, the program went on
to great critical acclaim and public success. Van
Dyke and Carl Reiner, the show's creator and driv-
ing force, ended their run while still successful in
1966.

The actor tried his hand at movies but returned
five years later with *The New Dick Van Dyke
Show,* which also had a TV setting: Van Dyke
played Dick Preston, a talk show host in Phoenix,

Arizona. The new show didn't achieve the success of its predecessor, and in its third season Dick Preston moved his family to Hollywood, where he starred in a fictional soap opera, *Those Who Care.* The move didn't help, and the program was canceled the following year. Two years later in 1976, however, he was back with a variety show, *Van Dyke and Company.* Although this show didn't last until the end of the year, it won an Emmy as the Outstanding Comedy-Variety or Music Series.

For the next few years Van Dyke appeared mostly in TV movies. His name didn't reappear in a title until 1988 with *The Van Dyke Show,* a short-lived sitcom in which Broadway star Dick Burgess retired to live with his son, Matt, who ran a small theater in Pennsylvania. Matt was played by Van Dyke's real-life son, Barry Van Dyke. Although this show also didn't make it until the end of the year, father and son were reunited in *Diagnosis Murder* five years later. Barry wasn't the only relative with whom Van Dyke performed. His brother, Jerry Van Dyke, guest-starred on *The Dick Van Dyke Show* as Rob Petrie's brother, Stacy, and on *The New Dick Van Dyke Show* as Dick Preston's brother, Mickey.

7. MARY TYLER MOORE

This former dancer first received notice in a show named for someone else—Dick Van Dyke. Mary

Tyler Moore played Rob Petrie's wife, Laura. Like most women on TV in the early sixties, Laura was a homemaker. After that show, Moore tried her hand at film but soon returned to TV. *The Mary Tyler Moore Show* in 1970 brought her even more attention than she had received in *The Dick Van Dyke Show*. Making a major break from Laura Petrie, Moore played Mary Richards, a single career woman working as assistant producer for the Minneapolis, Minnesota, local TV news. *The Mary Tyler Moore Show* became one of the best-loved TV shows ever, introducing characters such as neighbors Rhoda and Phyllis, producer Lou Grant, newswriter Murray, and empty-headed news anchor Ted Baxter. Moore's production company, MTM Productions, produced the series.

This show was a career high, and Moore has been unable to come close to matching it. She's made a valiant effort, however, starring in a number of shows, three carrying her name. In 1978, only a year after her show ended, she returned with *Mary,* a variety show. Among the cast were newcomers David Letterman and Michael Keaton, but *Mary* sank quickly, broadcasting only three episodes. Undeterred, Moore was back in less than six months with *The Mary Tyler Moore Hour*, a combination sitcom/variety show. She played variety show star Mary McKinnon; the sitcom portion presented *The Mary McKinnon Show*'s preparation, and the variety portion, the show itself. Only slightly more successful, it lasted three months. Moore left TV for a few years and had better luck in movies and on Broadway. She was on TV again in 1985 with another show called *Mary*. Returning to a newsroom context—this time for a daily tabloid—*Mary* was only slightly more successful than its predecessors and was canceled after four months.

8. STEVE ALLEN

Another television pioneer, Steve Allen had only four TV shows named for him, but his influence went far, far beyond that accomplishment. Allen's first national exposure was in 1950 with *The Steve Allen Show,* a live half hour on CBS every weeknight at 7:00. It lasted in that time slot for only a couple of months, then moved to weekday mornings at 11:30, where it expanded to an hour and stayed for the next year. He began hosting a local late-night show in New York in 1953, which went national on NBC as *Tonight!* in the fall of 1954. In one form or another, *The Tonight Show* has continued ever since. Although later hosts saw their name in the show's title, Allen did not.

His success in late night led in 1956 to a weekly NBC show against Ed Sullivan's successful Sunday evening variety program on CBS. This show was again called *The Steve Allen Show* and presented Elvis Presley's first national television appearance. Unlike Sullivan, *The Steve Allen Show* didn't limit its cameras to above Elvis's waist. Among the regulars were such comedy staples as Don Knotts, Bill Dana, Tim Conway, Louis Nye, Pat Harrington Jr., and Tom Poston, many of whom were making their first national appearances. *The Steve Allen Show* changed time slots and even networks, but it finally ended in 1961. Allen remained in the spotlight on TV, but his name returned to a program in 1967 for a summer variety series, *The Steve Allen Comedy Hour.* That same title appeared again on another NBC comedy/variety show in 1980 and 1981, in which Allen returned to a number of his classic bits and welcomed some of his former costars as guests.

9. JACK PAAR

Jack Paar was another figure from the earliest years of television. His first network show, in 1952, was the NBC game show, *Up to Paar,* where he asked contestants from the studio audience questions about current events. He next moved to CBS, where in 1953 he hosted another game show and a variety show, *The Jack Paar Show.* This program started on Friday mornings then moved to

Saturday evenings. After a short break to replace Walter Cronkite as host of *The Morning Show,* CBS's answer to NBC's *Today,* he was back in 1956 with *The Jack Paar Show* on weekday afternoons.

It turned out, however, that Paar's true forte was interviewing. When Steve Allen left *Tonight!,* NBC tried an unsuccessful magazine format with *Tonight! America after Dark,* and then turned to Paar, who stepped in to great success. That series became *The Jack Paar Tonight Show,* and Paar remained at the helm from 1956 until 1962. A volatile host, he wasn't afraid to cry over an emotional story or walk away from the show over a slight. When he finally left in early 1962, he apparently stayed on good terms with NBC, because he was back in the fall with a Friday-night hour of variety, *The Jack Paar Program.*

Paar continued to play to his strengths, recounting stories and chatting with guests. Highlights included Richard Nixon breaking the promise he made after losing the 1962 gubernatorial election ("You won't have Richard Nixon to kick around anymore") by playing an original musical composition on the piano, and the first American TV appearance of the Beatles in January 1964 (with a concert clip from the previous fall). Paar later admitted that he didn't know what he had in the Beatles clip—he showed it because he thought it was funny.

10. SONNY AND CHER

The name "Sonny and Cher" only appeared in two series titles, but between them the couple's names were in four. The married singers scored musical hits throughout the sixties, such as "The Beat Goes On" and "I Got You Babe." In 1971 they starred in *The Sonny and Cher Comedy Hour,* a summer variety show for CBS, and were picked up to continue in December. Each episode featured songs and good-natured banter between the couple. Cher's jokes usually focused on Sonny's short stature, while Sonny generally targeted Cher's nose. Unfortunately, as often happens in television, the loving rapport viewers enjoyed wasn't reflected behind the scenes. The duo's personal problems received more and more tabloid attention, and early in 1974, they filed for divorce.

The Sonny and Cher Comedy Hour was still in the top ten, so the networks scrambled to get these hot properties. Sonny kept most of the original production team and signed with ABC for *The Sonny Comedy Revue,* which premiered that fall. He tried to produce the same show, only now without Cher, but it just didn't work, and the series was canceled in December. *Cher* debuted the next

February, and although her ratings were huge at first, she couldn't maintain them. She also wasn't comfortable being responsible for a full variety show by herself. *Cher* survived for a year, but four weeks after her final program in 1976, she returned to the same time slot with Sonny again by her side. *The Sonny and Cher Show* started strong, but since the couple had reconciled only professionally and not personally, it was extremely awkward. The barbs and banter that had once seemed affectionate no longer did. Although *The Sonny and Cher Show* hung on for a year and a half, it was never the same.

4
Animal Magnetism

The animal world is quite different than our society, of course, but there's one thing that means success in both places: starring in your own TV show. Here are a few animals that have achieved that honor.

1. LASSIE

Lassie is undoubtedly the dean of animal TV stars. She (the character Lassie was a *she*, but all the collies that played her were *he*'s) starred in her own CBS series for eighteen years beginning in 1954, although she was the only constant throughout that time. Lassie started out with young boys as her owners—Jeff and Timmy were the first two—but she was later kept by a forest ranger. No dog as brave, selfless, and intelligent as Lassie could be "kept," of course, and by the end of the CBS run, Lassie was on her own, wandering the land and helping people or other animals in trouble.

2. GENTLE BEN

Most people have dogs or cats as pets, or maybe birds or fish. Not Mark Wedloe in the 1967 show *Gentle Ben.* His pet was a 650-pound black bear. Mark's father, Tom (played by Dennis Weaver; Mark was played by Clint Howard), was a wildlife officer in the Everglades, where there weren't a lot of other playmates nearby, but Mark didn't need them with Gentle Ben around. The two helped each other. Mark and his father saved Ben from poachers, and Ben looked out for Mark, as well. One important factor to remember, however, is that *Gentle Ben* is a TV show. Don't try to befriend black bears in real life—they're not really very friendly.

3. MR. SMITH

Don't let the nondescript name fool you. Mr. Smith was not a boring businessman. No, he was a superintelligent (IQ 256) talking orangutan who worked for the government. He had been Cha Cha, just a normal, run-of-the-mill orangutan that drank an experimental mixture that changed his life forever. The orangutan who played Mr. Smith in this 1983 sitcom was already a movie star, having costarred twice with Clint Eastwood (in *Every Which Way But Loose* and *Any Which Way You Can*) and once with Bo Derek (in *Tarzan the Ape Man*).

4. CHAMPION

Champion the Wonder Horse was best known as Gene Autry's trusty steed, but for a few months in 1955 and 1956 he had his own TV show, *The Adventures of Champion,* produced by his pal Gene. Autry didn't appear in the show, but instead Champion was owned by a twelve-year-old boy, Ricky North. Champion costarred with Rebel, a German shepherd. Between the two of them, they tended to keep Ricky out of trouble.

5. RIN TIN TIN

Rusty and his dog, Rin Tin Tin, the heroes of *The Adventures of Rin Tin Tin,* lived at Fort Apache, Arizona, in the Old West with the soldiers of the 101st Cavalry. Rusty had lost his family during an Indian raid, but he held on to Rinty and was ready to take his place with the troops as his newfound family. Although he was just a boy, Rusty was given the commission of corporal, though it was more an honorary title than an actual position. The show ran for five years from 1954 to 1959.

6. FLICKA

There are few stories as heartwarming as that of a boy and his horse. The 1956 series *My Friend Flicka* was also set in the West, at the Goose Bar Ranch in Montana. Ken McLaughlin lived on the ranch with his parents, Rob and Nell, and their ranch hand, Gus. Life could be hard on the ranch, and Ken and Rob had their share of conflict, but Flicka was always present as Ken's companion to help make life a little bit easier.

7. FLIPPER

Flipper was, of course, an incredibly intelligent dolphin that filled a role in the ocean similar to that of Lassie on land. Bud and Sandy Ricks were brothers, and their father, Porter, was the chief ranger of Coral Key Parks, Florida. Bud, the younger of the two brothers at ten years old, spent the most time with Flipper, but fifteen-year-old Sandy was never far away. Interestingly, the dolphin portraying Flipper from 1964 to 1968 in this series had the opposite problem of the dog playing Lassie: A female dolphin, Suzy, played the male Flipper.

8. BUTTONS

Although Buttons's name wasn't in the show title, the one chosen, *Me and the Chimp*, certainly got the idea across. Mike Reynolds was a dentist who lived in a lovely community in Southern California. Everything was going fine until his two children, Scott and Kitty, found Buttons wandering in the park. Naturally, they talked their parents into letting them keep the stray chimpanzee as a pet. Needless to say, hijinks ensued, but not for long. *Me and the Chimp*, which ran for only a few months in 1972, is renowned as one of TV's worst shows.

9. BOOMER

Cute little dog Boomer was the only regular character on 1980's *Here's Boomer*. Like Lassie before him, Boomer traveled far and wide, helping those in need. He had no owner to tie him down, no responsibilities holding him to any one place. Viewers were almost given special insight into what made Boomer tick, as the producers announced that new episodes would feature a voice-over of Boomer's thoughts. For whatever reason, after one episode in which we heard Boomer's thoughts, the idea was abandoned. The few remaining episodes after that time allowed Boomer his privacy.

10. **MISTER ED**

Although we may not have been privy to Mister Ed's actual thoughts, we were able to hear his voice on this series, broadcast from 1961 until 1965. Wilbur Post had moved into a new house, where he found the talking horse in the barn—just another perk of country living. Mister Ed and Wilbur used to have nice chats, but, unfortunately for Wilbur, Mister Ed refused to speak to anyone else, not even Carol, Wilbur's wife. He wasn't being obstinate; he just had nothing to say to other people. This obviously made things more difficult for Wilbur, but that wasn't exactly Mister Ed's problem, was it?

5
Games People Play

Sports were popular in the United States and around the world long before the invention of television, and they could survive just fine without it. But when TV gets added to the mix, sporting events can sometimes change. Televised football, basketball, and hockey games all have extra time-outs to make room for commercials. The mix of sports and TV can create some other oddities as well.

1. WRESTLING AND BOXING

Two sports that seemed made for early TV were boxing and wrestling. In those days broadcast equipment was large, bulky, and heavy, making it very difficult to move around. Both boxing and wrestling kept the action to a small area—the ring.

Camera operators could focus in on the ring and wouldn't have to make a move for an hour or three. In 1948, the first year that networks offered full prime-time schedules, boxing and wrestling accounted for thirteen hours of programming. Wrestling in particular, with its colorful heroes and villains, fit well on television. Of all the wrestlers during that time, Gorgeous George was the most flamboyant. He had long, golden hair, wore extravagant robes, contrived ostentatious entrances, and made the wrestling match much more of a production than a sporting event. Although Gorgeous George was not the first to stress the glitz and showbiz aspects of wrestling, he was by far the most successful. That success changed the course of wrestling and laid the groundwork for how sports would be covered on television.

2. THE HEIDI BOWL

It wasn't a college bowl game like the Rose Bowl, the Sugar Bowl, or the Orange Bowl. It wasn't even a planned event. The Heidi Bowl was a late-season game between two powerhouse teams of the American Football League. On November 17, 1968, NBC had set aside three hours of a Sunday afternoon to broadcast the game between the New York Jets and the Oakland Raiders. Following the game at 7:00, a new movie version of the classic Swiss story *Heidi* was scheduled to air. The game was exciting on all counts. Jets quarterback Joe Namath passed for 381 yards, while Raiders QB Daryle Lamonica threw for 311. Tempers ran high throughout the game—nineteen penalties were called for 238 yards. All those penalties made the game run long. The score was tied, but with a minute and five seconds left, the Jets kicked a field goal to go up 32–29.

At this point, 7:00, NBC cut away from the game to start the movie. Football fans were livid—so many phone calls flooded the NBC switchboard in New York that the phone system crashed. The fans were even more incensed when they discovered that the Raiders had scored two more touchdowns in the last sixty-five seconds, beating the Jets 43–32. Dick Cline, supervisor of broadcast operation control, switched the game off, but it wasn't his decision. Network policy stated that the prime-time schedule must start on time. Cline was later told that had he decided to show the end of the game and bump *Heidi,* he would have been fired. But this event caused networks to reconsider their rules, and within a few days it became network policy to show sporting events in their entirety, delaying the start of prime-time programming as long as necessary.

3. **THE "AGONY OF DEFEAT" GUY**

How would it feel to have one of the great catastrophes of your life on display for the whole world to see, broadcast week after week? Vinko Bogataj knows. He was competing for Yugoslavia in the 1970 International Ski Flying Championship in Oberstdorf, West Germany, just starting a jump, when he lost control and tumbled at great speed off the side of the ramp, resulting in a spectacular crash. Bogataj survived the plunge, but he was soon added to the opening of *ABC's Wide World of Sports,* providing the visuals while broadcaster Jim McKay intoned about "the thrill of victory and the agony of defeat." Safe at home as a truck driver in Yugoslavia, Bogataj didn't realize he had become a folk hero in the United States. During a *Wide World of Sports* anniversary show, Bogataj made a surprise live appearance, and the cream of the sports world gave him a standing ovation. According to producer Doug Wilson, even Mohammed Ali went home with an autograph.

4. THE 1972 MUNICH OLYMPICS

Sports reporter Jim McKay had to step out of his traditional play-by-play shoes during the 1972 Summer Olympics in Munich, West Germany, when eight Palestinian terrorists invaded the living quarters of the Israeli athletes. Although several Israeli Olympians escaped, two were killed almost immediately and nine more were held hostage. In the United States, the Olympics were being broadcast by ABC, and only sports reporters were on the scene. Middle East correspondent Peter Jennings was called in, but the bulk of ABC's broadcast was anchored by McKay.

Although the attack took place early in the morning of September 5, scheduled Olympic events weren't canceled until later in the day. But of course all eyes were on the black-hooded invaders on the balcony of the Israeli compound. Sports cameramen became news cameramen as West German police negotiated with the terrorists throughout the day. A deal was finally arranged for the terrorists to leave with their hostages and fly out of the country. Although initial reports out of Munich were that all the hostages had been rescued, that later proved to be incorrect. An ambush at the airport by German police didn't go as planned, and all nine Israeli hostages, along with five of the terrorists and one police officer, were killed. At the end of what had become a marathon broadcast, McKay, with grave understatement, announced, "They're all gone."

5. **BILLIE JEAN KING VS. BOBBY RIGGS**

The 1973 "battle of the sexes" tennis match between Billie Jean King and Bobby Riggs marked the coming of age of women's tennis. Riggs was a fifty-five-year-old former Wimbledon champion who proclaimed himself a "male chauvinist" and the scourge of women's tennis. In the early seventies, women's tennis didn't have the prestige or receive the attention of men's tennis, and Riggs wanted it to stay that way. King had already won Wimbledon several times by the time Riggs challenged her to a "winner take all" match. She had rebuffed his requests until he devastated her rival Margaret Court in two sets, 6–2, 6–1. Riggs's decisive win merely reinforced his arguments, so King felt she had to take him down a few pegs.

The hype for their match was overwhelming, and they met in front of thirty thousand spectators in the Houston Astrodome and more than forty million TV viewers. Borrowing a page from Gorgeous George's book, King and Riggs made spectacular entrances: A reclining King was carried by toga-wearing "slaves" onto the court in a Roman litter while other "slaves" fanned her with peacock feathers; Riggs entered in a rickshaw pulled by buxom models. The presentation was out of a three-ring circus, but when the match started, King dominated Riggs, winning 6–4, 6–3, 6–3. It sounds silly in the twenty-first century, but by taking Riggs to the cleaners, King proved that a woman was fit to compete against a man, and she put women's tennis on the map, where it started to receive the respect it deserved.

6. CARLTON FISK'S HOME RUN IN THE 1975 WORLD SERIES

In one of the most famous baseball clips in TV history, Boston Red Sox catcher Carlton Fisk hit a home run in extra innings to win game six of the 1975 World Series against the Cincinnati Reds. Although the ball certainly had the distance, it wasn't clear whether it would be fair or foul, so Fisk watched from the first base line, his hands waving the ball to stay fair. In its 1998 list of TV's greatest sports moments, *TV Guide* ranked this number one.

While the home run would have been good no matter what, the clip of Fisk waving the ball fair might never have happened. Harry Coyle was directing NBC's coverage of the game, and for this series in Boston's Fenway Park he had placed a camera in the left-field wall, Fenway's famed Green Monster. Coyle had instructed Lou Gerard, the camera operator inside the Green Monster, to follow the ball if Fisk hit it. As Fisk came to the plate, Gerard noticed a rat inside the wall, coming his way. Fisk hit the ball, but Gerard didn't follow it, because his eyes were on the rat. Gerard didn't move the camera, so it stayed on Fisk, capturing his body English and creating a baseball clip for the ages.

7. **THE 1989 WORLD SERIES EARTHQUAKE**

There are certainly events that transcend sports, but it's not often that one of those events happens during the middle of a sportscast. The 1989 World Series was called "The Bay Bridge Series," because it pitted the San Francisco Giants against the Oakland A's. Shortly before game three of the series at Candlestick Park, the San Francisco Bay area was hit by a 7.1-magnitude earthquake. Most of the TV cameras were focused on Candlestick Park, and since this was expected to be a sporting event rather than a news event, only sportscasters were on the scene.

As at the 1972 Munich Olympics, the broadcasters quickly exchanged their sports caps for news hats. The cable network ESPN, with Bob Ley handling the coverage, brought the first pictures of the quake to the nation, and ABC's Al Michaels dropped his usual play-by-play persona to supply news descriptions of the event. It was quite some time before any of the regular national news correspondents could get to the scene, so Michaels handled the coverage out of San Francisco for several hours. Although a previous Emmy Award winner for sports coverage, he was nominated for an Emmy in news coverage for his performance that night.

8. DAN JANSEN'S GOLD MEDAL

During the eighties and nineties, there was no more dominant figure in men's speed skating than Dan Jansen. Over his career he won twenty medals at the World Championships, and more than fifty World Cup medals. But an Olympic medal always eluded him. His first Olympics was in 1984, and he came home empty-handed, but he was still young. Tragedy struck during the 1988 games in Calgary, Alberta, Canada. His sister Jane died of leukemia the morning of his 500-meter race, and Jansen fell in both that event and the 1,000-meter. Jansen returned to the 1992 games, competing in fewer events so that he could concentrate. The best he could do in the 500-meter, however, was fourth place, just shy of a medal.

Speed skaters around the world were in agreement that Jansen was the best, and he came into the 1994 Olympics as the 500-meter world record holder. He had announced that he would retire after the games, so it would be his last opportunity for an Olympic medal. Jansen slipped once again in the 500-meter race, touching his hand to the ice for balance and slowing down enough that he fell to eighth place at the finish. It seemed like it was all over. He still had the 1,000-meter race, but he was not favored. Although he slipped slightly in this race as well, he skated to a new world record

JohnLeeMontgomeryIII/NouVeauPhoto.Net/Nashville,TN

After winning his gold medal for speed skating in the 1994
Olympics, Dan Jansen became sought after as a popular guest on
TV talk shows. Here he prepares for an appearance on
Prime Time Country, with producer Francesca Peppiatt.

and Olympic gold. The entire world had been root-
ing for him and was thrilled. As a demonstration of
this, CBS compiled a montage of Jansen taking
his victory lap with his nine-month-old daughter,
Jane, on his shoulder as announcers from a number of countries announced his victory in their own
language, each displaying the same amount of en-

thusiasm for his success as had the CBS announcers.

9. THE XFL

Football broadcasts are always big moneymakers for the networks, and when NBC lost the rights to NFL telecasts after 1997, it knew it had lost a cash cow. Over on cable TV, wrestling had experienced a resurgence, largely due to the efforts of World Wrestling Federation chairman and impresario Vince McMahon. Dick Ebersol, NBC Sports chairman, joined with McMahon to bring a wrestling attitude to football and create the Xtreme Football League (XFL). Promising a much rougher game than that provided by the NFL, the XFL also stressed scantily clad cheerleaders and open microphones on the sidelines (accompanied by censors with their fingers on the bleep buttons at all times). In February 2001, the XFL debut broadcast presented the New York/New Jersey Hitmen against the Las Vegas Outlaws and featured commentary by Minnesota governor and former wrestler Jesse Ventura.

The initial ratings were very promising, and McMahon quickly proclaimed himself the savior of television football. Ratings dropped by 50 percent the second week, however, and by the time the season reached its championship—what it called "The Big Game at the End"—they were off 75 percent from the first broadcast. The level of play on the field often wasn't up to professional level, which turned off football fans, and all the other bells and whistles weren't enough to bring in wrestling fans. After NBC and the WWF each lost about $35 million on the one season of the league, NBC canceled its broadcasts and the XFL folded.

10. *CELEBRITY BOXING*

Network executives seem determined to bring down the barriers between sports and showbiz, and they tried again in early 2002. The Fox Network reached back to the forties to return boxing to prime time. But instead of actual boxing matches, *Celebrity Boxing* pitted famous (or sometimes infamous) people against each other. Former child star Danny Bonaduce, who played Danny on *The Partridge Family,* squared off against Barry Williams, Greg from *The Brady Bunch.* Another former child star, Todd Bridges, Willis of *Diff'rent Strokes* fame, faced one-hit rap wonder Vanilla Ice, aka Rob Van Winkle.

The top draw, however, was former Olympian and felon Tonya Harding against presidential accuser Paula Jones. Jones was a late replacement for "Long Island Lolita" Amy Fisher, whose parole officer wouldn't approve the appearance. For the record, the winners were Bridges, Bonaduce, and Harding. Predictably, television critics decried the bad taste of the event, but just as predictably, the ratings were huge, putting it in a tie for Fox's highest-rated entertainment program of the 2001–2002 season. Given that, it was also predictable that Fox ordered more *Celebrity Boxing* specials.

6
Top of the Pops

One of the most effective ways of making a TV show identifiable and memorable is through its theme song. Recently the TV networks have become so desperate to keep viewers from clicking the remote that they've cut theme songs to a bare minimum. But there was a time when the songs that began and ended a show could be the highlight of the program. Some themes became so popular that they made the leap from the TV screen to the radio speaker. These TV theme songs ranked highest on the *Billboard* charts.

1. "THE BALLAD OF DAVY CROCKETT"
When Walt Disney's *Davy Crockett* was introduced, the character stormed the 1950s. Fess Parker, who played Davy, shot to stardom, and every

kid had to have his or her own coonskin cap. (The cap was so popular that even Estes Kefauver, U.S. senator and presidential candidate from Davy's home state of Tennessee, wore one.) Although many people believe Davy Crockett starred in his own series, he actually appeared in only five episodes of Disney's catchall program, *Disneyland*. Several different versions of "The Ballad of Davy Crockett" were rushed into release. Unfortunately for Fess Parker, his version followed the Bill Hayes recording into the stores and never caught up. Hayes's record hit number one and stayed there for five weeks in 1955. Parker didn't do too badly, however, reaching number five a few weeks later. A third version of the song, by country singer Tennessee Ernie Ford, entered the charts a week after Parker's record and also crawled up the charts to number five. Singer Hayes had another TV connection: He played Doug Williams on the soap opera *Days of Our Lives* beginning in the seventies.

2. "THE THEME FROM *S.W.A.T.*"

It may have been an unoriginal name for a song, but that didn't stop it from reaching number one in 1976. The TV show *S.W.A.T.* was the first time many Americans heard about this police unit. The initials S.W.A.T. stood for Special Weapons and

Tactics, and the team, led by Steve Forrest as Lieutenant "Hondo" Harrelson, favored military tactics to fight vicious and extreme crime that was too much for an ordinary beat cop. Produced by Aaron Spelling, *S.W.A.T.* was heavily criticized for its excessive violence, but that's what many of its fans tuned in to see. "The Theme from *S.W.A.T.*" was recorded by Rhythm Heritage, a group of Los Angeles studio musicians, and it appears on their album *Disco-fied,* along with "Keep Your Eye on the Sparrow," the theme from *Baretta,* which also made it to the top twenty.

3.   "WELCOME BACK" FROM *WELCOME BACK, KOTTER*

Gabe Kotter, the alter ego of *Welcome Back, Kotter* star Gabe Kaplan, had worked all his life to get out of the neighborhood where he grew up, but, sure enough, as soon as he became a teacher, he felt a responsibility to return to his alma mater to teach the remedial class, which was primarily made up of the "sweathogs." Vinnie Barbarino became the most notable "sweathog," providing the launching pad for the career of John Travolta, who appeared in the films *Carrie* and *Saturday Night Fever* while he was working on *Welcome Back, Kotter.* The theme song also welcomed back a familiar face in the form of composer and performer John Sebastian. Sebastian had been the leader of the Lovin' Spoonful in the sixties, and 1976's "Welcome Back" became his first number one hit since "Summer in the City" a decade earlier.

4. *"MIAMI VICE* THEME"

Just as the phenomenon of *Miami Vice* affected the television and fashion realms during the 1980s, it only makes sense that it would make its presence felt on the music scene as well. Sonny Crockett and Ricardo Tubbs wouldn't have seemed quite so stylish without the omnipresent mix of popular songs and Jan Hammer's background music on the soundtrack. It was inevitable that a soundtrack album would be released; when it appeared in 1985 it moved quickly to number one on the charts, taking over that territory for twelve weeks. The week after the album reached that peak, the show's theme song, written and performed by Hammer, hit number one on the singles chart.

5. **"HOW DO YOU TALK TO AN ANGEL" FROM** *THE HEIGHTS*

If you make a television show about a struggling rock band, it's only a matter of time until this band will start releasing records. It happened with the Monkees, it happened with the Partridge Family, and it happened again in the fall of 1992 with the Heights, the title band of this series. *The Heights* told the story of a diverse (of course) but mostly blue-collar group of kids following their dreams to become a chart-topping band. They got their wish, as the show's theme song rose all the way to number one on the real-world charts. Unfortunately, the series itself wasn't quite so fortunate. The week after the single hit number one, the series was canceled. One footnote to the series is that two of the actor/band members have gone on to more success on other shows. Charlotte Ross took her place as Detective Connie McDowell on *NYPD Blue,* and Alex Desert began to appear as Jake, the blind newsstand agent, on *Becker.*

6. "DRAGNET"

Police Sgt. Joe Friday was one of the most recognizable characters on television, and the theme to his show one of the most recognizable themes. The nine notes that introduced the criminals in each episode to their judgment and punishment have been parodied from the TV screen to the playground. Jack Webb and his costars played their characters so straight that at times they seemed to have no emotion at all. The program was hugely popular in the middle fifties, consistently ranking in the ratings' top ten. Webb brought the show back in 1967 to reach a whole new generation. The Ray Anthony Orchestra brought this theme all the way up to number two during the first incarnation of the series in 1953.

7. **"BELIEVE IT OR NOT"** FROM *THE GREATEST AMERICAN HERO*

He's walking on air. At least that's what the theme song to this light-hearted 1981 superhero show tells us. William Katt played high school teacher Ralph Hinkley, who had a close encounter with aliens in the desert. He was given a red supersuit that, once he put it on, gave him the powers to fly, turn invisible, and use X-ray vision. But what to do with these abilities? FBI agent Bill Maxwell (Robert Culp) had the answer—Ralph must fight crime! Ralph lost the instructions for his suit, however, so he had to figure out his powers as he went along. Joey Scarbury recorded this theme, which went all the way up to number two in the charts during the summer of 1981.

An unfortunate real-life coincidence plagued the show shortly after it went on the air. President Ronald Reagan was shot by would-be assassin John Hinckley. For the next little while, Ralph's student's called him only "Mr. H." When avoiding Ralph's last name altogether just wasn't feasible, the last name "Hanley" was dubbed onto the soundtrack. After a few months, however, he became Hinkley again.

8.   "SECRET AGENT MAN" FROM *SECRET AGENT*

The name of this theme song has caused some people to misremember the name of the series from which it came. The series itself was called simply *Secret Agent.* This is the second series in which Patrick McGoohan portrayed British spy John Drake. The character first appeared in the half-hour show *Danger Man,* then a few years later in the hour-long *Secret Agent.* Although more than one version of the theme appeared on record, Johnny Rivers had the big hit in 1966, reaching number three. The song itself complains that "they've given you a number and taken away your name." In *The Prisoner,* a series that followed *Danger Man* and *Secret Agent,* McGoohan played a former intelligence agent who was confined by persons unknown to a seaside village. Although McGoohan has claimed that *The Prisoner* was not a sequel to *Secret Agent,* the similarities are unmistakable. The character in *The Prisoner* was known only as Number 6, but at the beginning of each episode he insisted, "I am not a number; I am a free man!"

9. "HAWAII FIVE-O"

The Ventures were one of the great instrumental surf bands of the sixties, and if there were ever a program that deserved a great surf theme, it was *Hawaii Five-O*. Jack Lord played Steve McGarrett, who was the head of a unit of the Hawaiian state police answerable only to the governor. He led a crack team of both mainlander and Hawaiian detectives that kept Honolulu and Hawaii safe for the tourists. Shot entirely on location, this 1968 series showed off beautiful scenery, but it all seemed somehow wasted on the hard-boiled McGarrett. Each episode opened with a huge wave, reminding us that the surfers were never very far away. The Ventures employed their big guitar sound to carry the theme song to number four the year after *Hawaii Five-O* premiered.

10. "HAPPY DAYS"

This was a theme song that might never have happened. When the fifties sitcom *Happy Days* premiered in 1974, "Rock Around the Clock" by Bill Haley and the Comets appeared over the opening credits. Although this remained the theme for a time, it was ultimately replaced by a new song written specifically for the series. As Ron Howard and Henry Winkler brought their characters of

Richie Cunningham and the Fonz to a wide audience, more and more people heard the new theme song and wanted to have their own copy. In 1976 Pratt and McClain rode "Happy Days" to number five for the musical duo's only brush with the top forty.

7

Holy Oscar, Batman!

Between 1966 and 1968 one of the most sought-after roles on TV was as a Special Guest Villain on *Batman*. Airing on ABC, *Batman* was an odd show. For the kids, it was serious melodrama. For those a bit older, however, the series was absurd fun. Airing twice a week, every episode promised a rock-'em, sock-'em fight full of POWs and ZOWIEs. In a throwback to movie serials of the 1940s, every Wednesday night the week's celebrity villain would ensnare Batman and Robin the Boy Wonder in an ingenious deathtrap, but on Thursday—same Bat-time, same Bat-channel—the Dynamic Duo would escape and bring the villain to justice. Villains were allowed to "chew the scenery," and performers lined up for the chance. In a little over two years, *Batman* had more than its share of past and future Academy Award winners and nominees squaring off against the Caped Crusaders.

1. **SHELLEY WINTERS**

The true Academy Award heavyweight to take on Batman and Robin was Shelley Winters as Ma Parker. Patterned after the real-life outlaw Ma Barker of the thirties, Ma Parker was the head of a redneck crime family. In her more serious career, Winters won two Oscars, both for Best Supporting Actress, for the films *The Diary of Anne Frank* in 1959 and *A Patch of Blue* in 1965. Her performance in 1951's *A Place in the Sun* gained her a nomination for Best Actress, and, after running around in an upside-down ocean liner in 1972's *The Poseidon Adventure,* she was again nominated for Best Supporting Actress. *The Poseidon Adventure* also featured another Bat-villain, Roddy McDowell, who threatened the Dynamic Duo as The Bookworm.

2. **CLIFF ROBERTSON**

Only one Bat-villain won an Oscar for a performance he gave in the same year he appeared on *Batman.* Cliff Robertson won Best Actor for the 1968 film *Charly,* in which he played a mentally challenged man given enormous intelligence only to see it fade away. In 1968 on *Batman,* he had a return engagement as Shame, a stupid cowboy villain who didn't receive enormous intelligence. Robertson first appeared in 1966 as Shame, a takeoff of the Oscar-winning film *Shane.* He had such a good time with the character that on his return appearance he brought his then-wife Dina Merrill with him to join in the fun. Also participating in that second clash was another Oscar nominee, Hermione Baddeley, nominated for Best Supporting Actress in 1960 for *Room at the Top.*

3. ART CARNEY

When he appeared as The Archer on *Batman,* Art Carney was well known as Ralph Kramden's pal from *The Honeymooners,* Ed Norton. As the suave Robin Hood-type villain in the first episode of *Batman's* second season, he was almost unrecognizable to those who only knew him as a goofy second banana. Apparently academy voters were likewise impressed with Carney's range in 1975 when they awarded him the Best Actor Oscar for *Harry & Tonto,* the story of an elderly man and his cat hitchhiking their way west to find a new life.

4. ANNE BAXTER

Although several Bat-villains returned for multiple battles with the Caped Crusaders, only one guest star played two different villains in separate epi-sodes. In the first season, Anne Baxter appeared as Zelda the Great, but instead of a return appear-ance in the third season, she teamed up with Vin-cent Price's Egghead as Olga, Queen of the Cossacks, a character similar to Zelda the Great. Baxter won a Best Supporting Actress Oscar for playing a drug addict in 1946's *The Razor's Edge,* but she soon made her way to playing the kind of royalty she portrayed on *Batman,* appearing in 1956 as the conniving Egyptian princess Nefretiri, who had designs on Charlton Heston's Moses in *The Ten Commandments.* Possibly trying to corner the market on scheming and manipulation, Baxter may be best known for the Oscar-nominated role of Eve Harrington, the devious Broadway under-study who tried to maneuver her way to stardom in the 1950 film *All About Eve.* Both roles are cer-tainly appropriate training to play two different Bat-villains.

5. GEORGE SANDERS

All About Eve produced another Oscar-winning villain, George Sanders as Mr. Freeze. Sanders won the award for Best Supporting Actor for his performance as a Broadway critic in that film. Sanders's debonair, cosmopolitan style proved an apt match for Batman's earnest, straightforward view of the world. George Sanders had also been married to another Bat-villain, Zsa Zsa Gabor, who appeared as Minerva in the very last episode of the series. Unfortunately for Sanders, the thrill of challenging Batman and Robin was not enough. Although Mr. Freeze came back to oppose Batman twice more, neither of those appearances featured Sanders. A few years after *Batman* went off the air, George Sanders killed himself in Barcelona. His suicide note explained that he had become bored.

6. OTTO PREMINGER

Although Sanders didn't return to *Batman,* Mr. Freeze did, and he didn't lose any of his old-world aura. His second appearance was portrayed by a three-time Oscar nominee who was never nominated in any acting categories. Austrian-born Otto Preminger had acted from time to time (most notably in 1953 as the Nazi commandant in *Stalag 17*), but his primary career was as a director. He was nominated as Best Director for two films—*Laura* in 1944, and *The Cardinal* in 1963—and as producer of 1959 Best Picture nominee *Anatomy of a Murder*. As an indication of how hot a guest spot on *Batman* was, Preminger, who had known *Batman* producer William Dozier for a number of years, called the producer and begged him for a part. Mr. Freeze was Preminger's first time in front of the camera in more than a decade.

7. BURGESS MEREDITH

One of the villains who appeared most often against Batman was The Penguin. Although this is a role for which Burgess Meredith is well remembered today, he had a long career in film and television before The Penguin waddled across the screen. He played George in the 1939 Oscar-nominated film version of John Steinbeck's *Of Mice and Men,* but it wasn't until after his appearances on *Batman* that he received his own nominations. His first nomination for Best Supporting Actor came in 1976 for *The Day of the Locust,* with his second following the next year for another character that has stayed within the public's memory: Mickey, Rocky Balboa's trainer in the first *Rocky* film, a role he reprised in three of the four *Rocky* sequels. Unfortunately, neither of his nominations resulted in a win.

8. VICTOR BUONO

King Tut was another villain who appeared in a number of *Batman* episodes. The villain was a mild-mannered college history professor until a blow to the head made him believe he was actually the Egyptian pharaoh King Tut. Victor Buono

Photofest

To a generation of fans growing up in the sixties, Burgess Meredith
may be best known as the Caped Crusader's nemesis the
Penguin. By the time he first appeared on *Batman*, he'd had an
illustrious acting career. Meredith received two Academy Award
nominations in the seventies.

played a wide variety of roles in movies and television, but he received his Oscar nomination for Best Supporting Actor quite early in his career for the part of the singing teacher opposite Bette Davis and Joan Crawford in 1962's *What Ever Happened to Baby Jane?*

9.   CAROLYN JONES

Most famous for portraying the character of Morticia Addams in the TV version of *The Addams Family,* Carolyn Jones appeared twice on *Batman* as Marsha, Queen of Diamonds. Using a love potion that made men become her slaves, Marsha almost had Batman walking down the aisle with her. In her second chance against the Dynamic Duo, she teamed up with The Penguin, but the end result was no more successful. Jones had small roles in a number of films during the fifties such as *Invasion of the Body Snatchers, The Seven Year Itch,* and *The Man Who Knew Too Much.* Her Oscar nomination, however, came for a smaller film, *The Bachelor Party,* in 1958 (not the Tom Hanks film of the same name from the eighties). Her private life was also of some note—at one time Carolyn Jones was married to mega-producer Aaron Spelling, the man responsible for *Melrose Place, Dynasty, The Love Boat,* and *The Mod Squad,* among many others.

10. **GLYNIS JOHNS**

Batman was nothing if it was not a product of its time, but it wasn't the only trend out there in the sixties. One prime location for the birth of trends during the decade was swinging London, so it was only a matter of time until Batman paid the city a visit. Well, almost. Just as *Batman* was normally set in Gotham City rather than New York, Batman and Robin crossed the pond to Londinium rather than London. In the third season, Ireland Yard called upon the crime fighters to stop a crime spree by Lord Fogg and Lady Penelope Peasoup, played by Rudy Vallee and Glynis Johns. Although Glynis Johns may be best remembered as Mrs. Banks, the mother who hires Mary Poppins in the movie of the same name, she scored her Oscar nomination for Best Supporting Actress in 1961 for *The Sundowners,* a story set in the Australian outback.

8
Where Was That, Again?

When setting the scene for a TV show, one major component is location. Is the show set in a city, or the country? Is it a tropical island, or the frozen north? As soon as a TV show can establish its sense of place, it has lowered one more barrier to the viewers' understanding and enjoyment of the program. The fastest way to establish a location, of course, is to put it right front and center in the title.

1. **DALLAS**

The sweeping, sprawling story of the Ewing clan was as big as the state of Texas. It ran fourteen seasons from 1978 until 1991. The city of Dallas suggested cowboys, oilmen, and power, and that's just what this series gave us, with a modern twist.

Sometime during the Depression, wildcatter Jock Ewing had struck oil and turned his find into a multimillion-dollar enterprise. He had some skeletons in his closet from this period, and they were released little by little as the show progressed.

The audience's main concern was the modern-day soap opera of Jock's oldest son, contemptible, conniving J.R., played by Larry Hagman, and his schemes to maintain control over Ewing Oil. Viewers hated him, but they were also fascinated to see what he would do next. At the end of the third season, one of J.R.'s enemies gunned him down. No one was worried that he wouldn't survive—he was too good a character for the show to lose—but the question sweeping the country throughout the summer of 1980 was "Who shot J.R.?" The answer, finally revealed on the first show of the fourth season, brought in the largest audience for an episode of a series ever seen up to that time.

2. *BOSTON PUBLIC*

With its simple title, this show tells us two things: It takes place in Boston, and it's about a school. The school in question is Winslow High School, and this drama focused on the ups and downs faced by the teachers rather than, as is often the case with shows about school, the students. The series first aired in 2000, and since the action took place in the twenty-first century, the teachers had more to worry about than spitballs and talking in class. They had to fight for the respect of their students and deal with the violence and sexual innuendo that now seems a part of growing up. Behind-the-scenes intrigue among the teachers and staff was also present, complete with the political infighting that's a part of many workplaces.

3. *L.a. Law*

Producer Steven Bochco had just finished revitalizing cop shows with *Hill Street Blues*. For his next challenge, he decided in 1986 to try the same thing with lawyers in (guess where?) Los Angeles. Although *L.A. Law* had its share of courtroom scenes, the show was mainly interested in the interplay of the various partners and associates of McKenzie, Brackman, Chaney & Kuzak, a small downtown law firm. Until now, most TV lawyers had worked with a secretary and possibly an assistant, but rarely if ever an entire firm. Bochco took the audience behind the scenes to explore how the law was really practiced. The stereotypes were still there—fatherly senior partner Leland McKenzie, brash young lawyer Michael Kuzak, and slimy divorce specialist Arnie Becker, for instance—but it was all overlaid with a new sheen of realism.

4. *THE CHICAGO TEDDY BEARS*

Despite its title, this wasn't a show about friendly, gentle Chicago football players. Instead, this 1971 series was a situation comedy set in Prohibition-era Chicago. Linc McCray owned a speakeasy with his Uncle Latzi (played by John Banner, *Hogan's Heroes*' Sergeant Schultz), but of course things couldn't be as simple as that. Linc's cousin (and another nephew of Uncle Latzi) was Big Nick Marr, a small-time gangster who wanted in on the action. Uncle Latzi was sympathetic to his crooked nephew, but everyone else in the cast saw him for the ruthless hood he was. Despite its setting, *The Chicago Teddy Bears* was a comedy and didn't have the vicious violence of, say, *The Untouchables*. Sure, there were random tommy gun shootings from time to time, but it was all in good fun.

5. *NASHVILLE 99*

From the title, you might think you were looking at the name of a highway. Nope—it's a police badge number. Badge number 99 belonged to Det. Lt. Stoney Huff (his full name was Stonewall Jackson Huff), a member of the Nashville police department. Stoney investigated various crimes in Music City (well, not that many—the series didn't last over a month in 1977) and often ran into real-life country music stars making a cameo. Claude

Akins played Stoney; his partner, Det. Trace
Mayne, was played by country singer and actor
Jerry Reed.

6. *VEGA$*

No, Las Vegas isn't really spelled with a dollar sign
(though perhaps it should be), but the title gave
viewers a very quick feel for what kind of show
they would be watching: full of glitz, but with a
seedy underside. Dan Tanna, a handsome young
private eye played by Robert Urich, was the hero,
and somehow he found a murder to solve every
week. He moved among the high rollers in the ca-
sinos, the showgirls backstage, and the lowlifes on
the street. Between stops, he also made quite a
sight cruising the Vegas strip in his red '57 T-Bird
convertible. *Vega$* lasted three years, beginning in
1978.

7. *BAKERSFIELD P.D.*

Taking its cue from the tough police dramas of the
1980s and '90s, *Bakersfield P.D.* often opened its
episodes with police roll call. Observant readers
have already noticed, of course, that instead of a
big-city police department, this 1993 show was
set in Bakersfield, California. The pace was more
laid back here, the crimes far more mundane.
There was one remnant of a big-city police show,

Det. Paul Gigante (played by Giancarlo Esposito), a half-Italian, half-black transplant from Washington, D.C., who gradually got used to life in the slow lane. Smart and funny, *Bakersfield P.D.* was the kind of comedy that gave quirky a good name.

8.   *MIAMI VICE*

One of the hottest shows of the eighties, *Miami Vice* took its location very seriously. The show's entire look and atmosphere seemed to scream out *beach resort*. Everything, from Sonny Crockett's sports jackets on down, was sun-drenched in tropical pastels. Crockett, played by Don Johnson, and his partner Ricardo Tubbs, played by Philip Michael Thomas, may have spent most of their time undercover trying to catch drug kingpins, but they never let that interfere with the hedonistic spirit that inhabited Miami at that time. Did the show influence the city, or did the city influence the show? That may be a question for the ages, along with this little puzzler: Did Sonny Crockett even own a pair of socks?

9.   *THE STREETS OF SAN FRANCISCO*

Some TV shows just borrow the name of a city, but others fully inhabit their namesake. *The Streets of San Francisco,* which aired from 1972 until 1977, seemed to immerse itself in the character of that

city. The most obvious way it did this was through
car chases. It may have been done a million times,
but there's nothing like watching a car actually
leave the ground as it careens down the San Francisco hills toward the bay. Karl Malden played Det.
Lt. Mike Stone, a twenty-three-year police veteran
who was never without his trademark hat, and seldom without his trench coat. He was tough when
he had to be, but his generous heart was never far
away. Inspector Steve Keller was played by a
young Michael Douglas in one of his earliest
brushes with fame.

10. *WKRP In Cincinnati*

Behind the scenes at Midwestern radio station
WKRP (go ahead, sound out the letters) provided
a variety of crazy characters—Dr. Johnny "Fever"
Caravella (played by Howard Hesseman), the wild
morning DJ; Gordon "Venus Flytrap" Sims (Tim
Reid), the smooth nighttime man; Les Nessman
(Richard Sanders), the timid yet self-important
news writer; Herb Tarlek (Frank Bonner), the
pushy sales manager with a penchant for plaid;
and Jennifer Marlowe (Loni Anderson), the beautiful receptionist who always seemed like she was
really running the place. Most of the time *WKRP,*
which ran from 1978 until 1982, had little to do
with the city where it was set, but in one episode,

the producers really rose to the occasion to relate to Cincinnati. When several people were killed in a rock-concert stampede in the real Cincinnati, an episode of *WKRP* dramatized the morning after the concert to address the tragedy and memorialize the victims.

9
Small Screen to Big

Television shows have always seemed like kissing cousins to feature films. The sizes of the screens are different, of course, feature films always have much larger budgets, and TV shows must be made much more quickly, but the similarities between them are overwhelming. There's cross-pollination between the two as well. There's almost always a movie of some sort showing on TV, and old TV shows are often adapted into new movies. Every now and again, though, a TV show will come along that can exist as both a TV show and a movie. This doesn't refer to films like *Mission: Impossible* or *The Fugitive,* big-screen adaptations that bring in the top movie stars, make a few changes, and essentially replace the TV show. No, these are shows that jumped to the silver screen with their casts and concepts intact. They were essentially new episodes of the TV series on a much larger scale.

1. *STAR TREK*

The most successful of all the shows that jumped from small to large screen was *Star Trek*. The program had limped along in the ratings while it was on NBC from 1966 until 1969. In fact, it only survived into its third season because of a massive letter-writing campaign by fans. It had remained popular in reruns, however, and after the mega-success of *Star Wars* in 1977, a *Star Trek* reunion movie was given the green light. Everyone was back, including William Shatner as Captain James T. Kirk, Leonard Nimoy as Spock, DeForest Kelley as Dr. Leonard "Bones" McCoy, and James Doohan as Chief Engineer Montgomery "Scotty" Scott.

Star Trek: The Motion Picture appeared in 1979 and was just the first of six *Star Trek* movies that were made with the original crew of the Starship *Enterprise*. The second, 1982's *Star Trek II: The Wrath of Khan,* even brought back the villain from one of the TV episodes fifteen years earlier. The success of these movies brought a sequel series back to television in 1987, *Star Trek: The Next Generation*. After the original crew retired from movies, Captain Jean-Luc Picard and the *Enterprise* crew of *The Next Generation* left the broadcast airwaves and began to make movies of their own.

2. *POLICE SQUAD!*

Police Squad! spawned a series of movies that many fans may not even realize originated on TV. Filmmakers Jim Abrahams, David Zucker, and Jerry Zucker came out of nowhere with their hilarious 1980 film *Airplane!,* a spoof of the disaster movies of the 1970s. One of the most striking ideas in *Airplane!* was to take TV icons known for their straight-arrow portrayals of cops, spies, and other tough guys and encourage them to go crazy in shredding those images. After *Airplane!* took Hollywood by storm, the three movie creators expanded into television. The series they did in 1982, *Police Squad!,* starring Leslie Nielsen as the deadpan Frank Drebin (whose rank seemed to change from episode to episode), kept a very low profile with only six episodes before disappearing from the airwaves.

The three producers liked their concept, though, so they returned to the arena where they had previously tasted success. *The Naked Gun: From the Files of Police Squad!* brought Nielsen back as Drebin and was successful enough to inspire two sequels: *The Naked Gun 2¹/₂: The Smell of Fear* and *Naked Gun 33¹/₃: The Final Insult*. These films provided Leslie Nielsen with an entirely new career as a comedian. One of the side effects, however, is that watching any older performances from the serious phase of his career is almost impossible. For instance, just try to sit through *The Poseidon Adventure,* which features Nielsen as the captain of the doomed luxury liner, without expecting a goofy punch line.

3. *McHALE'S navy*

This World War II comedy surprisingly inspired two theatrical films while it was still on the air. The first movie, titled simply *McHale's Navy,* appeared in 1964 and brought Ernest Borgnine as McHale, Tim Conway as Ensign Parker, Joe Flynn as Captain Binghamton, and the rest of the gang along for the ride, along with George Kennedy and Claudine Longet. It was essentially a ninety-minute episode of the series, as the crew got caught up with gambling debts and had to raise money any way they could to pay them off, all the while thwarting Captain Binghamton (who might be better known by the nickname the crew gave him, "Old Leadbottom"). The second film, *McHale's Navy Joins the Air Force,* came out the following year and was somewhat of a departure from what had come before. McHale was nowhere to be found, but Parker, Binghamton, and many regulars from the crew were present. The trouble began as Ensign Parker was mistakenly believed to be a pilot in the air force. Neither of these movies should be confused with the 1997 remake that starred Tom Arnold and David Alan Grier.

4. *DRAGNET*

The first TV show to make the jump to movies was *Dragnet,* which pioneered the way in 1954. This ultrarealistic depiction of police work had already been a hit on radio and had made the transition to television fairly smoothly. The series based its episodes on actual cases from the Los Angeles Police Department. As he had on radio and would in the movie, Jack Webb played Sergeant Joe Friday, a character who couldn't possibly have been more by-the-book and straightforward. Webb was more than simply the star of the series, however; he was also the creator, producer, director, and usually writer. Although Friday had a number of partners throughout the run of the series, Ben Alexander as Sergeant Frank Smith settled in for the long haul.

Dragnet consistently rated among the top five programs after its debut in 1952, so it wasn't a huge leap to decide to take it into theaters. The longer running time allowed Friday and Smith to look more closely into the details of their case, which involved the brutal shotgun murder of a bookie. The Supreme Court's Miranda ruling was still more than a decade away, so Friday and Smith thought nothing of running roughshod over civil rights. *Dragnet* was the first of five feature films Jack Webb would direct. The series also inspired a parody movie in 1987 starring Dan Aykroyd and Tom Hanks.

5.   *THE MUNSTERS*

A sitcom about a family of monsters, *The Munsters* ran for two years during the mid-sixties. Herman Munster (played by Fred Gwynne) was the father, a Frankenstein-looking creature who worked in a mortuary. He was married to Lily (Yvonne DeCarlo), a vampire, and together they had a son, Eddie, a wolf-boy. Exactly how Frankenstein and vampire DNA combined to form a wolf-boy was never adequately explained. Rounding out the cast were Lily's father (played by Al Lewis), who held a strong resemblance to Count Dracula, and Marilyn, the glamorous blond niece who was something of an outcast, the "white sheep of the family."

Even though the show was canceled in the spring of 1966, a feature film was released later that same year. *Munster, Go Home* revealed that Herman had actually come from English nobility and had inherited the family title and manor. The Munsters moved to England as Herman became Lord Munster, the Earl of Shroudshire. Complications arose, however, when the family had to deal with the previous earl's other heirs. In an odd bit of trivia, there actually is a Lord Munster in English nobility, but he is the Earl of Munster, not Shroudshire.

6. *BaTMan*

Another TV show, which may have caused *The Munsters* to be canceled, came to the silver screen in 1966. Once *Batman* premiered at 7:30 Wednesday evenings opposite *The Munsters,* it caused such a sensation that *The Munsters* was gone within four months. The success of *Batman* caught almost everyone by surprise, but the producers were smart enough to get a feature film into the theaters while the Bat-craze was at its height. The screen is bigger, so everything else had to be bigger to match.

The movie introduced viewers to the Bat-cycle, the Bat-boat, and the Bat-copter. Also much bigger than the weekly half-hour series was the threat Batman and Robin faced: Four of their most vicious foes, the Joker, the Penguin, the Riddler, and

Catwoman, had teamed up as the United Underworld to kidnap the Security Council of the United World Organization. Almost all the normal stars of the series were on board. Adam West was Bruce Wayne/Batman, and Burt Ward was Dick Grayson/Robin, with Cesar Romero as the Joker, Burgess Meredith as the Penguin, and Frank Gorshin as the Riddler. The only replacement star was Lee Meriwether as Catwoman. The TV Catwoman, Julie Newmar, was shooting another film, *Mackenna's Gold,* and wasn't available.

7. *THE MONKEES*

American TV's answer to the Beatles, the Monkees were sometimes called the "pre-fab four." Producers Bob Rafelson and Bert Schneider put the group together from scratch in 1965 through open auditions. Mickey Dolenz and Davy Jones were both child actors coming of age, while Michael Nesmith and Peter Tork were aspiring musicians. Their show could have been the imagined result of the Beatles doing *Help* as a weekly series. The show was a hit with teens, and the Monkees soon started scoring their own chart hits, such as "I'm a Believer" and "Last Train to Clarksville."

After spending a weekend in 1967 tossing out ideas with the Monkees and his friend Jack Nicholson, Rafelson started on a movie. The result, titled

Head, was a disjointed and random series of events that in many ways encapsulated the sixties. Along with Schneider, Rafelson and Nicholson produced, and the two got the screenwriting credit (the Monkees have claimed they were denied the writing credit they deserved). Rafelson also made his film directing debut. The movie took longer than expected, and the Monkees' TV series was canceled before it came out, which helped make the film an absolute bomb at the box office. The Monkees slowly broke up over the next couple of years, but Nicholson and Rafelson each shot to success. In 1969 Nicholson appeared in *Easy Rider,* and the year after that Rafelson directed him in *Five Easy Pieces,* putting both their names permanently on Hollywood's map.

8. *GET SMART*

One of the funniest shows of the sixties, *Get Smart* made fun of the secret agent/superspy trend that followed in the wake of James Bond. Created by Mel Brooks and Buck Henry, *Get Smart* turned the genre on its head. In a time before every other person on the street had a cell phone, Maxwell Smart, Agent 86 (Don Adams), had his own portable phone in his shoe—unfortunately, he had to take his shoe off to use it, and it would ring at the most inopportune times. In virtually every episode his boss, played by Edward Platt and known only as Chief, very quickly became exasperated with Max's ineptitude. Max's partner, played by Barbara Feldon, also had no name, only a number: Agent 99.

Get Smart ran for five years beginning in 1965 and was resurrected as a feature film in 1980. Titled *The Nude Bomb,* the film featured Maxwell Smart saving the world from a madman who had a bomb that would not kill people but would make all their clothes disappear. With Leonard Stern, the executive producer and writer of the original show, on board, the movie looked to have potential. But Edward Platt, who had passed away a few years after *Get Smart* ended, was replaced by another actor, Dana Elcar, and Agent 99 was nowhere to be found in the movie. In the end, what had been so fresh and funny a decade earlier seemed long stale. *The Nude Bomb* is one film that lived up to its name.

9.   *TWIN PEAKS*

To say that film director David Lynch made offbeat films would be a gross understatement. His movies of the late 1970s and '80s, such as *Eraserhead, The Elephant Man,* and *Blue Velvet,* were lessons in the bizarre and surreal. When he agreed to create and produce a TV series, it was big news, and the first episode of *Twin Peaks,* a two-hour TV movie, certainly didn't disappoint. Viewers learned about the murder of Twin Peaks' high school homecoming queen. "Who killed Laura Palmer?" echoed through the TV audience during 1990, and FBI agent Dale Cooper (Kyle MacLachlan) was determined to find out. The narrative of *Twin Peaks* was far from linear, wandering all over the place and often teasing viewers by barely hinting at its plot twists. Although the first episode scored well in the ratings—it was the highest-rated TV movie of the year up to that point—many of those viewers quickly bailed. Those who stayed, however, were rabid. Laura Palmer's killer was revealed before the end of the year, but by that point many more questions had been raised than had been answered, and the series continued for a few more months.

When *Twin Peaks* was ultimately canceled a year after it premiered, neither David Lynch nor the fans of the show were quite ready to let it go. Almost immediately, Lynch began work on a *Twin Peaks* feature film. *Twin Peaks: Fire Walk with Me,* however, did not pick up the plot threads left dangling at the end of the last episode but instead presented a prequel, detailing the last week of Laura Palmer's life. Because there had been no murder yet, Agent Cooper barely appeared at all. Although this development was not unusual for David Lynch, the critics and the public were not pleased with what they saw.

10. *THE X-FILES*

A longer-lasting series that inspired the same kind of devotion as *Twin Peaks* premiered two years later in 1993. *The X-Files* followed the exploits of two FBI agents as they investigated unexplained events. Fox Mulder, played by David Duchovny, desperately wanted to believe these cases were paranormal, but down-to-earth Dana Scully, a medical doctor played by Gillian Anderson, would have none of it. There was a logical, scientific answer to everything, she believed, even if they weren't able to pinpoint what it was. As the series progressed, a larger, overarching plotline began to develop in the background. Mulder believed that, as a child, his sister had been abducted by aliens. Details emerged very slowly, but as they took shape it began to appear that a government conspiracy may have been responsible. With its two tag lines at the beginning of every episode, "Trust no one" and "The truth is out there," *The X-Files* became more and more paranoid. The ratings experienced a slow build, but series creator Chris Carter ultimately discovered that he had a cultural phenomenon on his hands.

In 1998, almost the middle of the series' nine-year run, Carter brought the whole production to movie theaters. The movie, titled *The X-Files: Fight the Future,* brought a number of plot threads over from the series and even included the death of a series character. The movie didn't clear up all the continuing questions, of course, and the series itself ran for four more years, asking new questions and raising new doubts.

10
A Good Slogan Is Forever

Although many people probably would prefer otherwise, we're never going to get television without the commercials. Love them (probably not) or hate them (most likely), they'll always be a presence among our favorite shows. Although many commercials are tedious, and sometimes it's not completely clear what product is being advertised, there are some commercials that can actually be entertaining. Some of the best commercials are those that have a particular catchphrase to help viewers remember their product. Over the years, a few of these catchphrases have caught on with the public to such an extent that they were used outside of the context of the products their commercials were advertising. Which of these commercial lines can still bring a smile to our faces?

1. "I CAN'T BELIEVE I ATE THE WHOLE THING."

Alka-Seltzer should be very pleased with its advertising agency over the years, as it has come up with one great line after another. This commercial started airing in 1971 and depicted a man in his pajamas sitting on the edge of the bed in obvious discomfort, repeating the line over and over. We've all had that feeling of overindulging, and we hope for his sake that the man on the bed has some Alka-Seltzer nearby. Some other Alka-Seltzer catchphrases include "Try it, you'll like it," "Mama mia, that's a spicy meatball," and "Plop, plop, fizz, fizz, oh what a relief it is."

2. "WHASSUP?"

First appearing late in 1999, this Budweiser catchphrase was repeated in a number of commercials and quickly made its way into the social lexicon as a way of greeting someone you hadn't seen in a while. In the first commercial, a group of guys talk on the telephone, each entering the conversation with his own rendition of "Whassup," each wilder than the version before. The first few commercials had a few other incidental lines of dialogue, but Budweiser quickly realized what it had and dropped them in favor of that one unforgettable word.

3.   **"THEY'RE GRRRREAT!"**

What's more natural than a tiger with a growl? Kellogg's used that idea to great advantage when coming up with a slogan for spokesman Tony the Tiger and Sugar Frosted Flakes. The catchphrase has been going since 1951, and it shows no sign of getting tired. Although the cereal has long been thought of as a children's breakfast food, in recent years Kellogg's has been trying to reposition it for adults as well. On the other hand, Kellogg's and other cereal manufacturers at some point became frightened of using the word "sugar" in connection with any children's food. Tony the Tiger now appears on boxes of Frosted Flakes (we can only guess what they might be frosted with).

4.   **"TASTES GREAT! LESS FILLING!"**

Some disagreements are just so basic that the sides can never get together. One such argument appeared in commercials for Miller Lite. In what started as a friendly conversation between former sports stars about the virtues of the beer, conflict always came between those who loved it because it tasted great and those who loved it because it was less filling. There could be no common ground. Although former jocks like Dick Butkus, Larry Csonka, Billy Martin, and Bob Uecker would almost come to blows over the issue, the ads maintained a spirit of good fun. This campaign produced more than two hundred different commercials and ran for over fifteen years, an eternity in the advertising world.

5. "FROM THE VALLEY OF THE JOLLY (HO HO HO) GREEN GIANT"

During the fifties and sixties, advertisers usually wanted to be cute. Why advertisers would think that consumers would want to buy frozen vegetables from a giant—and a *green* giant, at that—is anyone's guess. But when they made him a friendly, happy giant, gave him a laugh like Santa Claus, and added a catchy little jingle, it all seemed to come together. A successful brand name was born. There's not a person over age twenty-five—at least those who grew up with the television on—who can't sing along to that line.

6. "WHERE'S THE BEEF?"

Fast-food hamburgers have always been a competitive market. McDonald's is a worldwide brand name, so when relative upstart Wendy's came along, it had to do something to grab attention. Wendy's main selling point was the larger meat patties it used on its burgers, so it devised a commercial in which an old lady bought a hamburger from a competing fast-food restaurant, opened the bun to a tiny meat patty, stared straight into the camera, and demanded to know, "Where's the beef?" The question caught on to such an extent that presidential candidate Walter Mondale, criticizing a lack of content in President Ronald Reagan's policies, began to carry around a hamburger bun to ask that same question. The slogan was more effective for Wendy's than for Mondale, as history records Reagan winning reelection in a landslide.

7. "SORRY, CHARLIE"

Charlie the Tuna was the longtime cartoon spokesman for Starkist Tuna. In the famous commercial campaign, Charlie was always trying to get onto the Starkist fishing hooks so he could become a Starkist tuna. Why he had such a death wish was never quite clear, but it was always obvious that Charlie just wasn't good enough to join such a high-quality product. No matter what scheme Charlie might hatch, he was always rebuffed by a booming voice that said, "Sorry, Charlie," and explained how Starkist would only take the best tuna. Whether this was the voice of the fisherman on the surface or possibly the voice of God, "Sorry, Charlie" became an introduction to impending disappointment.

8. "I'D WALK A MILE FOR A CAMEL."

Before tobacco ads were banned from television in 1971, commercials for tobacco and cigarettes seemed to blanket the airwaves. A number of memorable slogans and catchphrases came out of these commercials, and one of the most successful was R. J. Reynolds's "I'd walk a mile for a Camel." A lone man looking for a Camel cigarette would wander into town, a hole in the bottom of his shoe from so much walking. He'd be offered other brands, but he was loyal to Camel, and would continue on his way until he found one. Although the question was implicitly raised, these commercials never explained why Camel cigarettes were so hard to find. They also never addressed why the man wore such cheap shoes that they would develop a hole over the short distance of a mile.

9. "IT TAKES A LICKING AND KEEPS ON TICKING."

Former newscaster John Cameron Swayze became the spokesman for Timex watches in this series of commercials, and he would oversee all sorts of damage to the watches. The most famous instance of abuse took the form of strapping it to the blade of an outboard motor and setting it in the water at full speed. At the end of the demonstration, Swayze would take the watch, hold it to his ear, and announce, "Still ticking." In the early years of this campaign, many of the demonstrations appeared on live TV, so there was no opportunity to fix it in editing if the watch stopped ticking or any other problem occurred.

10. "I'D LIKE TO TEACH THE WORLD TO SING . . ."

This commercial very effectively took the spirit of idealism that many shared during the late sixties and early seventies and turned it to selling soft drinks. A group of young people—ostensibly from all over the world—were gathered on a hilltop to sing about Coca-Cola as an engine of worldwide peace and harmony. The commercial was very powerful, developing tremendous public goodwill toward the Coca-Cola brand and cementing its reputation as not just an American soft drink, but a worldwide soft drink as well. The overarching Coca-Cola slogan that preceded this commercial, continued after it, and appeared in the backing vocals to this song, was just as memorable: "It's the real thing."

11
They Came from the Skies!

As long as humanity has been aware of the sky and the stars at night, we have wondered what else is out there. Are there other beings? And if so, are they like us? Space exploration and aliens visiting the Earth have long been staples of fiction in books, movies, and television, where the planet has been invaded by creatures from space countless times. Some of these creatures have been friendly and some have not. Most aliens have hidden themselves from the public, but a few have been completely up front about their intentions to conquer and enslave humanity. And a few have even starred in their own TV series.

1. *MY FAVORITE MARTIAN*

While on his way to cover a news story, newspaper reporter Tim O'Hara came across a crashed flying saucer, its sole occupant still alive. Naturally, instead of alerting the authorities, Tim took the alien home to nurse it back to health. After all, he could have a real scoop here! Although he looked human, it turned out the alien was from Mars. Tim adopted him, telling his landlady and others that his "Uncle Martin" had come to live with him. Instead of pursuing his scoop, Tim agreed to help Uncle Martin fix his flying saucer so he could return home.

Uncle Martin had a few enhanced abilities, such as the power to turn invisible and move objects through telekinesis. Before he could use these powers, however, his retractable antennae (which looked strikingly like a pair of rabbit ears for TV reception) rose out of his head. Although other people, particularly the landlady's boyfriend, Detective Bill Brennan, sometimes became suspicious, Tim and Uncle Martin were able to maintain their secret. Ray Walston played Uncle Martin in this 1963 series, with Bill Bixby as Tim.

2. *THIRD ROCK FROM THE SUN*

This crew of four aliens came to study the Earth and its culture. Although in their normal bodies (which we never saw) they looked nothing close to human, they were able to assume human form so they could mingle unnoticed with the population of Earth. The crew took up identities as a Midwestern family. The high commander became the head of the family, Dick Solomon, a physics professor at an Ohio university. The security officer, a lieutenant and second in command of the crew, took the form of a woman as Dick's sister, Sally Solomon. Since the lieutenant was male in his original form, Sally sometimes had trouble in expressing her femininity. The communications officer became Harry Solomon, the ne'er-do-well brother. Finally, even though he was actually older than the high commander, the remaining crewmember became Dick's adolescent son, Tommy Solomon, in order to study human puberty.

Although their alien identities were never found out, it goes without saying that the foursome did not always blend smoothly into their human surroundings. Dick, played by John Lithgow, struck up a romance with his office mate, Dr. Mary Albright, played by Jane Curtin. The aliens were sometimes visited by their supreme leader, the Big Giant Head, who also took human form during his visits to Earth and was played by William Shatner. *Third Rock from the Sun* ran from 1996 until 2001.

3.   *MORK & MINDY*

The alien Mork first visited Earth from his native planet Ork during the fifties, when he dropped in on Richie Cunningham on *Happy Days* (which actually aired in 1978). The audience responded so well to Mork that he returned to Earth later that year in a series set during the present day, landing in Boulder, Colorado. Fortunately, Mork also looked human, so he was able to fit into society fairly easily. He befriended a young woman, Mindy McConnell (Pam Dawber), and lived in her apartment.

Because Mork was portrayed by Robin Williams, things got weird on a fairly frequent basis. This was the public's first major exposure to Williams, and they apparently liked what they saw, as *Mork & Mindy* rocketed into the top ten and Williams established a successful and wide-ranging career. As the series progressed, Mork and Mindy fell in love and were married. Things worked backwards on Ork, so Mork spawned an egg from his belly button, which ultimately hatched into a huge middle-aged man with the mind of a child. This child, whom they named Mearth, was played by Jonathan Winters, who had been something of a mentor to Williams in real life.

4. *THE INVADERS*

Not all the aliens that TV has brought to Earth have been friendly and funny. This paranoid and suspenseful series from the late sixties presented its aliens as behind a secret conspiracy to invade and take over the Earth. Roy Thinnes played David Vincent, who had witnessed the landing of a spaceship but was never able to obtain unequivocal proof and as a result had very few places to turn. The aliens had come from their own dying planet and intended to conquer and colonize Earth.

Because, like most TV aliens on Earth, they could take human form, Vincent was never sure who he could trust and who was out to get him. A telltale sign that sometimes distinguished aliens from real humans was a misshapen hand with fingers slightly out of place, but Vincent always seemed to notice that at the most inopportune times. He was constantly on the run and could never tell whether he was making any headway against the aliens or not. In many ways, *The Invaders* was a forerunner of *The X-Files* (in which the aliens were so well hidden that it wasn't always clear whether they even existed at all). Certainly David Vincent would have found a kindred soul in Fox Mulder.

5. *ALF*

Finally, here was an alien that didn't look like a human being. Perhaps taking its cue from *E.T.*, ALF is an acronym, standing for Alien Life Form.

Looking more like a sort of aardvark than anything else, ALF was actually a puppet, unless he needed to walk around, in which case he was a little person in an ALF suit. ALF didn't want his presence on Earth to be known for all the usual reasons, so the Tanner family helped keep him in hiding. He had crash-landed his spacecraft into their garage, stranding him on Earth. That was probably just as well, however, as his home planet of Melmac had just exploded and, well, he didn't have anywhere else to go.

Although ALF got along with most of the family all right, he was a constant source of irritation for Willie Tanner, played by Max Wright. Wright, who performs the edge of exasperation better than perhaps anyone else, has appeared in a number of TV shows and movies doing a similar routine. *ALF* was on the air for four years from 1986 to 1990, and while it flirted with the top ten, it never became a breakout hit. It was the kind of show that no one would admit to watching at the time, but is fondly remembered in retrospect.

6. *MEEGO*

Another alien that mistakenly showed up in the backyard of a suburban family was Meego, brought to the small screen by Bronson Pinchot. He also looked like a human being, and the Parker kids, whose yard he landed in, took an immediate liking to him. Meego had a variety of useful powers he could show off, such as telekinesis, the ability to make time run more slowly or more quickly, and the ability to change shape into other living organisms. Although Meego originally intended to return to his home planet of Marmazon 4.0 as soon as he could repair his spaceship, he liked the Parker family enough that he decided to stay on for a little while as their babysitter and caretaker.

Dr. Edward Parker (Ed Begley Jr.), the father who was bringing up his family alone, was never aware of Meego's actual background—that secret stayed with the kids. He was just happy that he had found a babysitter his kids would accept. Surely all kinds of hijinks were bound to ensue from such a wacky situation, but the television audience never got a chance to see them. *Meego* was canceled after only six episodes in 1997.

7. *V*

Returning to the malevolent aliens, *V* depicted an Earth that had already been invaded by beings from another planet. *V* was short for Visitors, an alien race that had previously been introduced in two miniseries in 1983 and 1984. In those miniseries, the Visitors had tricked humanity and replaced Earth's governments with their own power structure, but they were overthrown by a small band of human rebels. Although the Visitors had appeared human, they were ultimately revealed to be a sort of giant lizard.

The Visitors' leader, a vicious ice queen named Diana, was played by Jane Badler. As the weekly series began in the fall of 1984, she was about to go on trial (reminiscent of the Nuremberg trials after World War II) for crimes against humanity. With the help of some human traitors, she escaped and regained control of Earth, viciously eliminating those who had resisted her. You can't keep a good human being down, of course, so naturally the small band of rebels again took up arms to overthrow the Visitors. Marc Singer, as former TV newscaster Mike Donovan, led the rebels.

As one way to demonstrate both their evil and their reptilian nature, the Visitors ate live mice. In almost every episode, Badler and her cohorts enjoyed this delicacy. In actuality the mice themselves were chocolate, but they were somehow too large to go down in one gulp. The actors were often shown with a mouse's tail slipping through their lips like spaghetti.

8. *ALIEN NATION*

Adapted from the 1988 feature film *Alien Nation*, this 1989 series portrayed a different sort of invasion from space. A slave ship carrying aliens from the planet Tencton had crashed in the Mojave Desert, and an entirely new population was added to the southwestern United States virtually overnight. Although the Newcomers, as they were called, were more intelligent and stronger than humans, they had no desire to conquer the planet and instead simply wanted to assimilate. They looked similar to humans, but the Newcomers' craniums were larger and covered with mottled skin rather than hair. They took American names and tried to move into regular jobs and responsibilities, but they faced fierce opposition.

In form, *Alien Nation* was a cop show, and it followed Detective Matthew Sikes (Gary Graham), an L.A. cop who was partnered with Detective George Francisco (Eric Pierpoint), the first Newcomer to attain that rank. Matt was the usual tough cop playing the singles scene on his time off, while George was a suburban family man. *Alien Nation* was clearly set up to examine the issue of racism without the historical baggage that usually attends that subject.

Midway through the series, the producers introduced an unusual plotline. George and his wife, Susan (Michele Scarabelli), were having a baby. However, Newcomers didn't reproduce the same way humans do. The fetus was carried by Susan during the first part of the pregnancy, but after a certain period of time, it was transferred to George, who carried it to term.

9. HARD TIME ON PLANET EARTH

Who knew that being banished to Earth could sometimes be a punishment meted out by alien judges to the most troublesome elements of their society? That's exactly what happened in 1989 on *Hard Time on Planet Earth*. An alien who had been born and bred to be a warrior was suddenly deemed too violent for his society, so he was exiled to Earth until, essentially, he learned some manners. The alien took the name Jesse when he arrived on Earth and took human form. He was accompanied by a parole officer of sorts, a sentient, orb-shaped computer named Control. Control was along to give Jesse help and guidance when he needed it, although Control's grasp of the customs and traditions of Earth left quite a bit to be desired as well.

Even though Jesse looked like a human, as portrayed by Martin Kove he retained his warrior's build and strength, so he was always a brute force to be reckoned with. Although he generally meant well, Jesse didn't necessarily help whatever situation he wandered into each week.

10. *SOMETHING IS OUT THERE*

The X-Files told us that the truth is out there, but that's not quite what this series had in mind. Like *V, Something Is Out There* began as a miniseries. Maryam d'Abo played Ta'ra, the mind-reading alien medical officer of a spaceship that had been invaded and taken over by a vicious space monster. Ta'ra escaped the ship to come to Earth, only to discover that the monster had already arrived.

As all TV aliens ultimately seem to do, Ta'ra came to Los Angeles, where she met up with a cop named Jack Breslin (Joe Cortese). Breslin helped Ta'ra track down the space creature, defeating it by the end of the 1988 miniseries. When the story resumed as a weekly series a few months later, Ta'ra and Breslin were free to protect the Earth from other potential alien invaders or just to fight crime in general. Even though Ta'ra was an alien, she looked like a beautiful, sexy woman, and she and Breslin felt some attraction to each other. Her interest ended at Breslin's hands, as hands were the primary focus of sexual activity on Ta'ra's planet. This caused no end of frustration for Breslin, of course, who also had to contend with Ta'ra's mind-reading abilities, which made his mind, and all the desires and fantasies therein, an open book to her.

12
It's Like Grand Central Station

When the two-man crew of the S.S. *Minnow* left Hawaii for their ill-fated three-hour tour, they weren't expecting to be stuck in a TV series for the next three years. Although the producers shot fewer than one hundred episodes, through the magic of after-school reruns, 1964's *Gilligan's Island* became one of the most popular, long-lasting, and well-known shows in TV history.

For those whose memories may be failing, a quick rundown of the cast: First mate Gilligan was played by Bob Denver, and the Skipper by Alan Hale Jr. The millionaire, Thurston Howell III, and his wife, whom he affectionately called Lovey, were brought to life by Jim Backus and Natalie Schafer. Movie star Ginger Grant was portrayed by

Tina Louise, the Professor by Russell Johnson, and Mary Ann Summers by Dawn Wells.

With all the ingenuity that the castaways showed in coming up with day-to-day items, such as a pool table, a battery recharger, and a car, it's amazing that they couldn't repair the two-foot hole in the *Minnow* or build a new boat. And for an uncharted island no one even knew existed, it sure got a lot of visitors. Throughout the show's run, the island received more than two dozen people who came and went while Gilligan and company stayed put. Here are some of the most notable.

1. WRONGWAY FELDMAN

The first guest star on *Gilligan's Island* was Hans Conreid as world-famous aviator Wrongway Feldman. Feldman, who had mysteriously disappeared ten years earlier, had actually crash-landed on this deserted island and had been living there ever since. The castaways helped Feldman repair the plane and get off the island, but, not earning the name "Wrongway" for nothing, he was never able to identify the location of the island for rescuers.

Feldman actually returned to the island later in the first season. Civilization had changed too much in the time he'd been gone, becoming too noisy and hectic, and he realized that he preferred the solitude he had enjoyed on a "deserted" island.

Using the kind of logic to which they would return again and again, the castaways decided to make the island itself too noisy and hectic so that Feldman would return to civilization for a rest. Indeed, they succeeded in alienating Feldman even further, forcing him to leave in search of another island that really was deserted.

2. **A JAPANESE SOLDIER**

Vito Scotti played a Japanese sailor who had spent the last several decades in a one-man submarine. His radio hadn't worked since 1942, so he had no idea that World War II had been over for most of that time. After coming ashore in the lagoon, he did what any good sailor would do on a new island: He conquered it. While most of the castaways were locked in a makeshift prison cell, Gilligan saved the day. Unfortunately the sailor himself got away, along with his sub, which had represented a way off the island.

Scotti, instantly recognizable to TV viewers for the several dozen guest star parts he played in programs ranging from *Bewitched* and *Mad About You* to *Gunsmoke* and *The Bionic Woman,* was the most frequent guest on *Gilligan's Island*. He later returned as the Japanese sailor in a flashback episode and appeared twice as mad scientist Boris Balinkoff, once switching the castaway's brains and later making them into mindless robots intended to rob Fort Knox. In neither of the castaway's encounters with the mad scientist did they successfully use his sophisticated equipment or luxury yacht to return to civilization.

3.　A JUNGLE BOY

It turned out that Wrongway Feldman had not been the only other inhabitant to share the island with the castaways. A jungle boy, played by a young Kurt Russell, had been there since before they had arrived. There was no indication where he had come from or where he had found the leopard-skin loincloth he wore, because the jungle boy could only communicate in grunts. He introduced Gilligan to the island's natural helium fountain (contrary to popular belief, many uncharted islands have one).

The castaways sewed their raincoats together for a makeshift balloon, but before they could decide who would ride the balloon for help, the jungle boy took it himself. On the radio they later heard that the boy had been found by an aircraft carrier, but because he had no spoken language, he couldn't tell the sailors about the castaways.

4.　THE MOSQUITOS

Not the Beatles but, the producers hoped, close enough, the Mosquitos (Bingo, Bango, Bongo, and

Irving) were the biggest band in the world. They were so big, in fact, that they had to find a deserted island upon which to escape their fans and get some rest. The island they found wasn't deserted, of course.

Sensing another possible rescue, the cast-aways tried a number of ways to ingratiate themselves with the Mosquitos in the hopes that the group would help them off the island. Getting into the spirit of the sixties, the men and the women started their own pop groups. Although the men were horrible, Ginger, Mary Ann, and Mrs. Howell were pretty good—so good, in fact, that the Mosquitos feared their competition and snuck off the island without them. The Mosquitos were played by Les Brown Jr. (his father was Les Brown of the Band of Renown fame) and The Wellingtons, the trio who sang the *Gilligan's Island* theme song each week.

5. ERIKA TIFFANY SMITH

No sixties sitcom was complete without a visit from Zsa Zsa Gabor, and *Gilligan's Island* was no different. Zsa Zsa played Erika Tiffany Smith, a wealthy socialite who wanted to buy the island in order to build a luxury hotel. While scouting the island, she fell in love with the Professor. Finally making a deal with Mr. Howell to buy the island (how he came to have the deed is never quite clear), she agreed to rescue them and returned to her yacht, but the rescue boat she promised to send from her yacht was thwarted by a storm and never arrived. When she returned to civilization and told her story, the authorities couldn't decipher the mix of English and Hungarian in her log (apparently there's never a Hungarian translator around when you need one).

6. VARIOUS DOUBLES OF THE CASTAWAYS

Against all odds, the island was visited three times by a double of one of the castaways. First was Thurston Howell's double. Claiming to be the rescued millionaire back in civilization, he took over Howell's business interests, selling them for quick cash. Taking a restful cruise, he accidentally fell off the yacht and made his way to the nearest island—we all know which one that was. His subterfuge was so convincing, however, that even Mrs. Howell couldn't tell him from the real thing. When he was found out in the real world, the fake Howell swam away from the island. With far better luck than the castaways themselves, he was rescued but never revealed what he knew about the island.

Gilligan's double, a Russian spy, was the next to show up, determined to discover what secret project the castaways were working on. Capturing

Photofest

The castaways of *Gilligan's Island* were isolated from civilization, but they weren't as lonely as one might expect. Twenty-nine of the series' ninety-eight episodes featured guest stars.

Gilligan, the spy took his place to learn what he could. No one believed Gilligan about the double after Gilligan escaped imprisonment, so he had to confront the double alone. The spy was ordered home by his government, however, and left the island without much incident. Assuming the others still wouldn't believe him, Gilligan kept it to himself.

The final double was Eva Grubb, an unattractive, mousy woman who had left civilization behind because men ignored her. Trying to help her out, the castaways gave her a makeover, discovering that she looked exactly like Ginger. With that revelation, she took her boat, left the castaways behind, and resumed Ginger's movie career.

7. HAROLD HECUBA

The world-famous movie producer Harold Hecuba, played by Phil Silvers, was scouting locations for future projects when he crash-landed into the sea by the island. He came ashore and proceeded to have the castaways do his bidding, treating them as his personal flunkies. Ginger explained that this was simply what movie producers did and convinced the others to go along with it so she could get in his good graces and work with him in the future.

After Ginger approached Hecuba in several different guises in her own audition of sorts, Hecuba rebuffed her. Wanting to raise Ginger's spirits and show off her talents as well, the castaways decided to stage a musical for Hecuba. The only scripts they had on hand were the Professor's books of Shakespeare, so they performed a musical version of *Hamlet*. Hecuba was impressed, but when he was rescued in the middle of the night, he left a note claiming he didn't want to wake anyone. The castaways later heard over the radio that Hecuba's next film project would be a musical version of *Hamlet.*

8. NORBERT WILEY

Don Rickles came ashore in a motorboat as Norbert Wiley, a career thief who wanted to escape the temptations of civilization. Before anyone knew he was there, he kidnapped various islanders and held them for ransom. When the castaways finally captured him, Ginger, taking on the role of a psychoanalyst, determined that Wiley's crime was a result of his troubled upbringing. They decided to reform him and return with him to civilization. Convinced that he was rehabilitated, the castaways threw a party to celebrate Wiley's new life. Wiley, however, sadly not reformed, took the diversion as an opportunity to steal everything of value to the castaways and return to the outside world alone to resume his life of crime.

9. GEORGE BARKLEY

Over thirty years before *Survivor,* the castaways experienced a similar backstabbing episode themselves. Strother Martin played George Barkley, a contestant from the game show *Take a Dare,* who would win $10,000 if he survived for a week on a deserted island. Landing on this island was a stroke of luck, because Barkley could survive simply by stealing the castaways' food and provisions.

He was ultimately discovered by the castways, who pled with him to get them off the island. He had a radio transmitter from the game show, and a simple word broadcast over it would save them. But saving them, of course, would mean losing his $10,000. Howell offered him $1,000,000 instead, but Barkley turned him down, thinking it was a scam. After arranging his pickup at the end of the week, Barkley threw his transmitter over a cliff, preventing the castaways from using it again and costing him his win. Barkley was rescued but didn't win his money, which had been hidden in the transmitter. Strother Martin later became known for a famous line from the film *Cool Hand Luke*: "What we have here is a failure to communicate." That was certainly true in this episode.

10. JONATHAN KINCAID

Rory Calhoun, famous for tough-guy roles in Westerns, played big-game hunter Jonathan Kincaid, searching out new prey to hunt. Based on the much-copied Richard Connell short story "The Most Dangerous Game," it was obvious that once he discovered the castaways, he would want to hunt one of them. Kincaid promised to save the castaways if Gilligan survived as his prey for twenty-four hours. No one was happy with the arrangement, but given that Kincaid had the rifle and they didn't, the castaways had little choice. With the help of his friends, Gilligan stayed alive for the full twenty-four hours, and good as his word, Kincaid ended the hunt, defeated. Unfortunately, Kincaid could not keep his promise of rescue. After all, if anyone discovered he had been hunting humans, they would lock him up and throw away the key.

Although they didn't get off the island, the castaways had the last laugh, as Kincaid couldn't psychologically accept his failure to capture Gilligan. Returning to civilization, he broke down, babbling the name Gilligan over and over, and was locked away anyway. Kincaid's assistant, Ramoo, was played by Harold Sakata, better known as Oddjob from the James Bond movie *Goldfinger*.

13
The More the Merrier

Television is a very fickle industry. Some performers work most of their lives toward a break that never quite comes. But there's a flip side to that phenomenon as well. When the industry takes a liking to someone, that goodwill can be hard to break. There are some performers who keep showing up on new TV programs year in and year out. No matter what happens, these performers are invited back for more, popping up not just as guest stars, but as regular cast members of new series.

1. ROBERT URICH—15

The all-time champ for the most TV series was Robert Urich, who powered past his competition. Although a household name, he never had that one hit to shoot him into the TV stratosphere, but he was part of the cast of fifteen different shows looking for it.

In his first series, *Bob & Carol & Ted & Alice,* he starred as Bob Sanders, with Anne Archer as his wife, Carol. This 1973 sitcom was based on a 1969 movie that explored the new, freer mores of sixties suburbia. The show didn't last three months, but Urich was back a year and a half later as Officer Jim Street in *S.W.A.T.* Street was part of the S.W.A.T. team of the title, and the gig lasted until the summer of 1976. The next fall saw Urich star in *Tabitha,* a spin-off from *Bewitched* that featured Darren and Samantha Stephens's daughter, Tabitha, a witch herself, all grown up and working at a TV station. Urich played the empty-headed newscaster, Paul Thurston. At the same time, he also appeared in *Soap,* a controversial sitcom that made fun of soap operas.

From the farce of *Soap,* Urich took a right turn into the role of hard-boiled detective Dan Tanna on *Vega$.* He had a chance to catch his breath there, as *Vega$* ran for three years. After a year without a series, Urich returned in 1982 with the underwater espionage show *Gavilan,* starring as former CIA agent Robert Gavilan, a consultant in oceanography. *Gavilan* lasted only a year, but in 1985 Urich was back with *Spenser: For Hire. Spenser* tied with

Vega$ for Urich's longest-running series. Filmed in Boston, it brought Robert B. Parker's one-named, quotation-spouting, highly principled private eye to life.

After appearing in the miniseries *Lonesome Dove,* Urich was back on a regular series payroll in 1990's *American Dreamer.* He played Tom Nash, a hotshot network-TV reporter who relocated to small-town Wisconsin after the death of his wife. The year after that he again played a father whose wife had died in *Crossroads.* In it he and his son motorcycled across the country, helping people along the way. That series rode quickly into the sunset, but the next fall, in 1993, in Urich returned to romantic comedy with Faye Dunaway in *It Had to Be You.*

Urich's next series was 1996's *The Lazarus Man,* a Western. He played an amnesiac in 1865 searching to learn his identity. This show came to an early end, however, when Urich was diagnosed in the summer of 1996 with a rare form of soft-tissue cancer. Although he believed he could continue the series, the producers decided to pull the plug. Urich immediately began treatment, but he refused to leave the public eye. While undergoing chemotherapy (which left him bald), he hosted *Vital Signs,* a documentary series about medical emergencies. During this time he also hosted the

PBS series *Boatworks,* which focused on people and their connection to boats and life on the water.

Urich's cancer went into remission, and he returned to series acting in 1998. *Boatworks* served as a nice stepping-stone to the updated and retooled *Love Boat: The Next Wave,* where he starred as Captain Jim Kennedy III. In the fall of 2001, Urich returned to sitcoms in *Emeril,* costarring as Jerry McKenney, the famous chef's agent. *Emeril* was canceled before the end of the year. Sadly, Urich unexpectedly succumbed to his cancer in April 2002 at age fifty-five.

2. HARRY MORGAN—11

A few TV stars have plateaued at eleven series. The first to reach that level was Harry Morgan, who held the record until Urich passed him. Morgan was acting long before TV was a fixture in most living rooms, and by the time he appeared in his first series, he had made more than fifty movies, including classics like *High Noon* and *The Glenn Miller Story.*

His first brush with series TV was on 1954's *December Bride* as next-door-neighbor Pete Porter. Pete complained about his nagging wife, Gladys, who was sometimes heard but never seen. Gladys finally showed up when Pete was spun off into his own show, *Pete and Gladys.* That show ran two years, and in 1963 Morgan turned around to join the cast of *The Richard Boone Show,* an anthology series that told a different story each week. The same actors, which included Robert Blake, Guy Stockwell, and Lloyd Bochner, appeared week after week but lasted only one season. Not one to sit on his laurels, Morgan took on *Kentucky Jones* in 1964. Dennis Weaver played Jones, a veterinarian with a California ranch. Morgan was his handyman, Seldom Jackson.

Following *Kentucky Jones,* which also lasted only a year, Morgan stepped into one of his most recognizable parts in 1967: Bill Gannon, Sgt. Joe Friday's partner on an updated *Dragnet.* Friday was played by Jack Webb, who also produced the program. No matter what crime confronted the partners, they were unflappable—some might say wooden. *Dragnet* lasted three and a half years, and in 1971, a year after it ended, Morgan was back in another Webb-produced show, *The D.A.,* playing Chief Deputy District Attorney "Staff" Stafford, supervisor to Robert Conrad as Deputy D.A. Paul Ryan. The series survived only into January of 1972, but in October of that same year, Morgan was reunited with Richard Boone in *Hec Ramsey,* a turn-of-the-century Western in which he played the town doctor, Doc Amos Coogan.

After *Hec Ramsey* had been off the air for a

year, Morgan took on his most successful role, that of Colonel Sherman Potter in *M*A*S*H,* a series about a Mobile Army Surgical Hospital in Korea. He remained there for eight years, longer than the Korean conflict itself had lasted, until 1983. Even after *M*A*S*H,* Morgan continued as Colonel Potter in *AfterMASH,* the spin-off that followed him and other *M*A*S*H* characters Corporal Klinger and Father Mulcahy to a Missouri veterans hospital.

AfterMASH made its last appearance in December 1984, but Morgan came back for another series only a year later with *Blacke's Magic.* Hal Linden played Alexander Blacke, a retired magician who turned his skills to thwarting crime, with Morgan as his father. That series ended only six months after it began, leaving Morgan free in 1987 to star in *You Can't Take It with You,* a series adapted from the Pulitzer prize-winning play and Academy Award-winning movie about a family of eccentrics.

3. **BETTY WHITE—11**

Betty White was a veteran of radio who made a smooth transition to TV. Her first starring role was as the title character in *Life with Elizabeth* in 1952. Elizabeth was married to Alvin, and the series revolved around the couple and their friends. For a

Betty White

Although she started her career in radio, Betty White has been a fixture on TV for more than fifty years. She starred in several TV series and served numerous times as the TV host for Pasadena's annual *Tournament of Roses Parade* on New Year's Day.

few months, White also hosted a lunchtime talk show, *The Betty White Show,* at the same time. (This is not counted among her eleven series, which focus on prime-time series.) When *Life with Elizabeth* finished production, White became a panelist on *Make the Connection,* a game show in which celebrities guessed how various contestants were connected. Another sitcom followed with *A Date with the Angels* in 1957, with White again playing half of a young couple. When that show was canceled, she held on to the time slot with a reincarnation of *The Betty White Show,* this time with a variety format. It lasted only a couple of months.

White's career took an interesting turn in the sixties, as her primary appearances were as a guest panelist on game shows. It worked out well when she met her future husband, Allen Ludden, the host of *Password.* They were married for eighteen years, until his death. In 1973 White agreed to guest star in one episode of *The Mary Tyler Moore* show as the man-hungry Sue Ann Nivens, a guest spot that turned into a four-year run until the series ended. Her image had always been virtuous and wholesome, and playing against type here was very effective. After *The Mary Tyler Moore Show,* she was back with the third go-round of *The Betty White Show*, this time as a sitcom.

She played Joyce Whitman, an aging Hollywood actor playing a tough street cop in the fictional series *Undercover Woman.*

White returned in 1985 with what may have been her biggest show, *The Golden Girls,* as naive and not-always-so-bright Rose Nylund. Originally cast as Blanche Devereaux, White wanted a change from man-hungry parts and asked for Rose instead. After *The Golden Girls'* seven-year run, White continued with Rose into a spin-off, *The Golden Palace,* in which she, Blanche (Rue McClanahan), and Sophia (Estelle Getty) took over a Miami hotel.

As soon as *The Golden Palace* was canceled, White joined the cast of *Bob,* which starred Bob Newhart as a comic book and greeting card artist. White played Sylvia Schmitt, the owner of the greeting card company where Bob worked. The show was canceled after only five of White's episodes. She returned in 1995, costarring as Marie Osmond's mother in *Maybe This Time.* Series number eleven came along in 1999 in the guise of *Ladies Man.* British actor Alfred Molina played Jimmy Styles, a contractor whose life was overwhelmed with women: his wife, Donna (Sharon Lawrence); his two daughters; his mother, Mitzi (White); his mother-in-law, Peaches; and his ex-wife, Claire. This show ran until 2001.

4. CLORIS LEACHMAN—11

Joining the eleven-series club in 2001 was Cloris Leachman, whose career encompassed a vast array of programs and genres. Along the way she won seven Emmy Awards. In 1949 she was a regular on the game show *Hold It Please,* acting out questions for contestants to answer. Leachman's first regular series role was as Effie Perrine, secretary to the lead character in 1950's live drama *Charlie Wild, Private Detective.* During its year and a half on the air, *Charlie Wild* was on three different networks: CBS, ABC, and DuMont.

Leachman served a brief stint on *Bob and Ray,* the comedy variety series starring Bob Elliott and Ray Goulding. The show ran from 1951 until 1953, but Leachman appeared only during the summer of 1952. Her next series stop was in 1957 as Ruth Martin, Timmy's adopted mother on *Lassie.* Unfortunately, that show was recast the next year, and only Timmy and Lassie remained. June Lockhart replaced Leachman as Ruth.

While raising her own family, Leachman did a lot of guest spots in the sixties, but took no long-term commitments. She changed that somewhat in 1970 as Phyllis Lindstrom on *The Mary Tyler Moore Show,* although even then she wasn't in every episode. Phyllis was Mary's flaky friend and landlady. After Lars, the character's husband, died in 1975, Phyllis left for her own spin-off, *Phyllis*, moving to San Francisco to live with her mother-in-law. When that show ended two years later, Leachman focused her energies on films, building quite a comic reputation with her appearances in Mel Brooks's movies. But it was back to her own series again in 1986, as she stepped in to replace Charlotte Rae, whose character, Mrs. Garrett, was leaving *The Facts of Life*. Leachman was introduced as Mrs. Garrett's sister, Beverly Ann Stickle. Staying two years until the end of that series, she watched Blair, Tootie, Natalie, and Jo grow to adulthood and move away.

Her appetite for series work whetted again, Leachman came back in the fall of 1989 with a Mel Brooks hotel sitcom, *The Nutt House*. She played two roles: Ms. Frick, the housekeeper with a thick foreign accent, and Mrs. Edwina Nutt, the hotel's owner. Six episodes later, the show was over. In 1991 she had more success with *Walter & Emily,* playing Emily Collins to Brian Keith's Walter Collins. The older couple was saddled with the upbringing of their grandson. Leachman's tenth series, *Thanks,* seemed like a bad idea from the start. Seeking humor among the Pilgrims in 1621 Massachussets, *Thanks* was labeled "Puritan fun" by CBS. It wasn't. Leachman began her eleventh series in 2001, *The Ellen Show,* playing Dot Richmond, the mother of Ellen DeGeneres's character. This show was cancelled in 2002.

5. **ROBERT CONRAD—10**

In his very first series, Robert Conrad set the tone for much of his career. In 1959 he played hip, cool detective Tom Lopaka in *Hawaiian Eye.* Although the show wasn't shot in Hawaii, it captured the laid-back mood of a swinging single crime fighter working in paradise. That smooth, cool exterior never strayed very far from Conrad and was prominently on display in his next and most famous series, *The Wild Wild West.* It mixed the mid-sixties secret agent trend with the still popular Western genre. Conrad played Jim West, who, along with master of disguise Artemis Gordon (Ross Martin), traveled in a specially outfitted railroad car. After a five-year run from 1965–1970, Conrad returned with a series more down-to-earth: *The D.A.,* a Jack Webb production, in which he starred with Harry Morgan. The show lasted less than six months, and Conrad was back in the fall as another undercover agent, this time shot in present-day Vienna. On *Assignment Vienna,* he played Jake Webster.

Conrad remained in the employ of the U.S. government in his next series, 1976's *Baa Baa Black Sheep,* the real-life story of World War II flying ace Major Gregory "Pappy" Boyington and his misfit squadron in the South Pacific. After that two-year run as a marine pilot, Conrad returned to fighting crime in *The Duke* as Oscar "Duke" Ramsey, an over-the-hill prizefighter who had found a new mission as a detective. This show ran only a month and a half in the spring of 1979, and in the fall of that year he tried again as *A Man Called Sloane*. Returning to familiar ground, Conrad starred as Thomas Remington Sloane III, the top secret agent for UNIT, which was in an eternal struggle with the evil KARTEL. It was never explained what either of these acronyms stood for.

Conrad didn't return to another series until 1988, with *High Mountain Rangers*, which started another trend for him. As Jesse Hawkes, he oversaw high adventure as the semiretired founder of a search-and-rescue team in the Sierra Nevada Mountains. Conrad's real-life sons, Christian and Shane, played Jesse's sons, Matt and Cody. These rangers stayed on the air for only six months, but the Hawkes family relocated to San Francisco in *Jesse Hawkes,* where they used their mountain tracking skills as detectives and bounty hunters. This series was canceled faster than *High Mountain Rangers,* but Conrad couldn't shake the mountains. In 1995 he starred in *High Sierra Search and Rescue*. Although it had no overt connection to *High Mountain Rangers,* the similarities were quite apparent. This time the head of the Sierra Nevada search-and-rescue team was named Tooter Campbell. The show itself would have benefited from a rescue of its own, as it didn't even last for two months.

6. ED ASNER—10

Although Ed Asner made his first TV appearance on *Naked City* in 1958, he didn't gain wide recognition until his second series, 1970's *The Mary Tyler Moore Show.* His first series was *Slattery's People,* a 1964 political drama starring Richard Crenna as James Slattery, an idealistic representative in a state legislature. Asner was the political reporter at a local newspaper.

Asner worked mostly in obscurity until *The Mary Tyler Moore Show,* in which he played Mary's boss, news producer Lou Grant. After that show's extremely successful run, Asner continued with the character for another five years. Fired with the rest of the newsroom at the end of *Mary Tyler Moore,* Lou Grant moved to Los Angeles to work as city editor for a daily newspaper on his own hour-long drama, *Lou Grant.* Asner provided continuity that allowed viewers to believe he was the same character on both shows, even though the tone of the two programs was completely different.

After *Lou Grant,* Asner went on to a succession of short-lived series. *Off the Rack* survived for about six months in 1984. Asner was Sam Waltman, the head of a garment factory who was forced to work with the widow (Eileen Brennan) of his deceased partner. As Principal Joe Danzig of the Bronx's Benjamin Harrison High, Asner had more success with *The Bronx Zoo,* airing from spring 1987 until summer of 1988. Asner next joined the cast of *The Trials of Rosie O'Neill* in its second year. His character, Walter Kovatch, was a retired cop and a die-hard conservative, a bit of a stretch for the outspokenly liberal actor. After *Rosie O'Neill* ended in early 1992, Asner was back in the fall on *Hearts Afire,* a romantic sitcom starring John Ritter and Markie Post and set in the office of a U.S. senator. Asner appeared as George Lahti, the ex-con father of Post's character. In its second season the series retooled and Asner was out, but six months later he had another show, *Thunder Alley,* playing Gil Jones, a retired stock-car racer and successful garage owner whose divorced daughter and three grandchildren move back in. Haley Joel Osment played one of the grandchildren. Premiering in the spring of 1994, *Thunder Alley* ran off and on until the summer of 1995.

In 1998 Asner was back with two different sitcoms. The first was *Ask Harriet,* another newspaper show, in which a fired male sports reporter returns in drag as a woman named Sylvia to write an advice column. Asner played the owner of the paper, "Old Man" Russell, who had eyes for Sylvia. *Ask Harriet* lasted only a month, but a month after that Asner was back with *The Closer* featuring Tom Selleck. As Jack McLaren, Selleck owned an advertising agency, and Asner was Carl "Dobbs" Dobson, his creative director. Although this was Asner's tenth series, it only lasted nine episodes.

7.   BRIAN KEITH—9

Another actor who held on to a tough-guy image for most of his career was Brian Keith, who had his first regular series in 1955. *The Crusader* was an overtly political show during a time when politics stayed mostly in the background. Keith's character, Matt Anders, was a freelance writer who helped people escape from Communist countries, trying to undermine Communism one person at a time. Keith left the present day for the Old West in his next series, 1960's *The Westerner.* As Dave Blassingame, he played a cowboy roaming the Southwest. The series was produced by Sam Peckinpah, who later built a reputation making hyperviolent movies such as *The Wild Bunch* and *The Getaway.*

The Westerner was canceled after thirteen weeks, but in 1966 Keith returned with *Family Affair,* the series that gave him his most recognizable character. Bill Davis, a confirmed bachelor, was a successful engineer. His enviable lifestyle, residing in a luxurious Manhattan apartment with his man-servant Mr. French, played by Sebastian Cabot, was broken when his brother and sister-in-law were killed in a car accident and Bill took in their children, the adorable six-year old twins, Buffy and Jody, and their teenage sister, Cissy. *Family Affair* became quite popular and lasted five years.

Keith followed up this success the next year with another show featuring kids. In *The Little People* he played pediatrician Sean Jamison, who, with his pediatrician daughter, Anne (Shelley Fabares), operated a free clinic in Hawaii. In its second year the show changed its name to *The Brian Keith Show.* There were no kids, though, in 1975's *Archer,* in which Keith played detective Lew Archer from the novels of Ross Macdonald. Archer used his mind rather than muscle to solve crimes.

When Keith returned to the series grind in 1983, it was as tough former judge Milton C. Hardcastle. Retired from the bench and no longer constrained by pesky legalities and regulations, Hardcastle decided to fight crime on the streets. The show was called *Hardcastle & McCormick,* and his partner was Mark "Skid" McCormick, a racing-car driver and ex-con. Only a year after the end of *Hardcastle & McCormick,* Keith was back in a sitcom, *Pursuit of Happiness,* as history professor and writer Roland Duncan. This show, which ran for about three months, should not be confused with 1995's *The Pursuit of Happiness,* a lawyer sitcom that ran for only two months.

Keith's next sitcom, *Heartland,* lasted only a few months in 1989 and featured the actor as B. L. McCutcheon (almost rhymes with "curmudgeon"), an opinionated farmer forced to move in with his daughter, son-in-law, and their three teenage kids. In 1991 Keith appeared in his ninth and final series, *Walter & Emily,* playing another grandfather, Walter Collins, with Cloris Leachman as wife Emily.

8.   TIM CONWAY—9

Tim Conway has had a long career as a second banana, providing laughs for other people's shows but never successfully carrying his own. He first came to the attention of Steve Allen, who made him a supporting player on *The Steve Allen Show* during its final year, in 1961. In the fall of 1962 he began the long-running role of Ensign Charles Parker on *McHale's Navy.* As Parker, the no-nonsense but bumbling officer sent in by Captain

Binghamton (Joe Flynn) to tighten up the loose ship run by Lieutenant Commander McHale, Conway perfected the type of character that would become his comedy staple.

Five months after *McHale's Navy* sailed into the sunset, Conway returned in his first starring series, *Rango,* a Western sitcom in which he played a bumbling Texas Ranger. Although *Rango* didn't last the year, Conway returned with another series, *The Tim Conway Show,* in January 1970. This sitcom featured Conway as Spud Barrett, the pilot for the one-plane Anytime Anyplace Airline. He was reunited with Joe Flynn as airline owner Herb Kenworth, but the show had completed its run by June.

Although he was hardly a roaring success, Conway returned in September with *The Tim Conway Comedy Hour*. This variety show featured such future stars as McLean Stevenson and Sally Struthers, but it was canceled even more quickly than the previous sitcom. Next followed a number of guest appearances on *The Carol Burnett Show,* which turned into a job as a full-time cast member in the fall of 1975. He stayed until that show left the air four years later. Conway had a knack for ad libbing and surprising his costars, who were often unable to maintain their composure on camera. He had such success here that he received his own show in 1980, again called *The Tim Conway Show,* this time produced by Burnett's husband and producer, Joe Hamilton. It was another hour-long variety show (cut to half an hour after a couple of months). The third time Conway's name appeared on a series wasn't the charm, and the show jumped on and off the schedule before finally biting the dust.

Not to be deterred, however, Conway was back in spring 1983 as an inept detective in *Ace Crawford, Private Eye.* Crawford, basically a comic version of Humphrey Bogart's Sam Spade, didn't even last a month. A few years later, Conway took a stab at a *Candid Camera* type of show, *Tim Conway's Funny America.* He traveled the country in disguise and caught interactions with the people he encountered on a hidden camera. Again the show was short-lived, airing for about a month and a half.

9.   TIM REID—9

Tim Reid began his TV career as a sketch comic in variety shows. The first, *Easy Does It . . . Starring Frankie Avalon* was a summer show starring the sixties heartthrob, which ran four weeks in 1976. The next summer Reid reprised his backup role for another variety show, *The Marilyn McCoo & Billy Davis Jr. Hour,* starring the singing duo who had been part of The Fifth Dimension. In the fall of the same year, Reid was part of the controversial *Richard Pryor Show*. Pryor, a cutting-edge comic who took the subjects of race and sex head-on, had a stormy relationship with NBC and fought intensely with the censor. The network had been willing to agree to only ten episodes, but after four both Pryor and NBC had had enough.

Reid came back in the fall of 1978 in his first continuing role as Venus Flytrap, the smooth late-night soul DJ on *WKRP in Cincinnati.* He remained on the show for its four-year run, and only six months after it ended joined the cast of *Teachers Only,* a high school sitcom that mostly took place in the faculty lounge. The show was canceled three months after Reid came aboard, so he was free to join *Simon & Simon,* an hour-long detective show that had already been on the air for two years. A.J. (Jameson Parker) and Rick Simon (Gerald McRaney) were brothers with very different styles working together as private detectives. Reid played their police contact, Detective Downtown Brown, who didn't mind bending a few rules to get what he needed.

Reid left *Simon & Simon* in 1987 for his first starring role on the series *Frank's Place,* a show he also executive produced. A critics' favorite, *Frank's Place* was set in a New Orleans restaurant and featured Reid as Frank Parrish, a Renaissance history professor from Boston who inherited the place from his long-lost father. Also in the cast was Reid's wife, Daphne Maxwell Smith. The show captured the slow and easy ambiance of New Orleans but failed to attract viewers and was gone after one season. Undeterred, the Reids came back just a year later as a sort of modern Nick and Nora Charles in *Snoops*. Chance Dennis was a professor of criminology, while his wife Micki worked at the U.S. State Department, and they had a knack for solving crimes. Another show with a quick turnaround, it didn't make it until the end of the year. Reid had more success with his next show, 1994's *Sister, Sister,* playing Ray Campbell, who had adopted one half of a set of twins separated at birth. The fourteen-year-old twins, Tia and Tamera (played by Tia and Tamera Mowry), reunited, pulling together Tamera's widower father and Tia's widowed mother Lisa (Jackee Harry).

10. RON RIFKIN—9

Ron Rifkin has one of those faces people think they've seen before but can't quite place. The nine series he has regularly appeared in, both comedy and drama, have provided him with a variety of characters. *Adam's Rib,* a 1973 series based on the 1949 Spencer Tracy-Katherine Hepburn movie, featured married lawyers. Adam Bonner (Ken Howard) was an assistant district attorney, and Amanda Bonner (Blythe Danner), an attorney for the defense, who often found themselves across the courtroom aisle from each other. Rifkin played Assistant DA Roy Mendelsohn. They didn't have long to work together, however, as the show was canceled in just three months.

Rifkin next went to Mel Brooks's 1975 Robin Hood farce *When Things Were Rotten*, playing the evil Prince John against Dick Gautier's Robin. Even with the Mel Brooks pedigree, however, the show didn't round up viewers and was gone in December. In spring 1978 Rifkin appeared in his third short-lived series, *Husbands, Wives & Lovers,* from another high-profile name. Joan Rivers created this continuing story about a group of five couples in the suburban San Fernando Valley near Los Angeles. Unlike other nighttime soaps, this one was an hour-long sitcom. The audience didn't take to it, and it also survived for only three months.

Rifkin's next assignment had a higher profile. *One Day at a Time* had been on the air for five years when Rifkin joined the cast and was a bona fide hit. He played Nick Handris, an artist who partnered with series lead Ann Romano (Bonnie Franklin) to become a freelance advertising team.

The professional relationship turned romantic, but it only lasted a year, when Nick was killed in a car wreck before the 1981 season. His next role was a left turn into drama, as Rifkin passed through the cast of *Falcon Crest,* the continuing wine country saga starring Jane Wyman and Robert Foxworth. During the 1983–1984 season, he was featured as Dr. Lantry.

He next showed up as a series regular on *The Trials of Rosie O'Neill* in 1990. The title character, played by Sharon Gless, was a successful lawyer who gave up private practice to join the public defender's office. Rifkin portrayed the head of that office, Ben Meyer. Rifkin remained a dramatic actor in *ER,* coming in during the 1995–1996 season as Dr. Carl Vucelich, a distinguished surgeon who ran into trouble when he was discovered faking his test results. That didn't do much for Rifkin's character, who quickly disappeared from the show.

He continued his career with another medical role, this time with a slight twist. In 1997's short-lived *Leaving L.A.,* he played Dr. Neil Bernstein, the idiosyncratic chief medical examiner in the Los Angeles Coroner's Office. The year 2001 saw Rifkin in the much-talked-about show *Alias.* He appeared as Arvin Sloane, the director of the nefarious SD-6, a spy agency initially thought to be a rogue cell of the CIA but discovered to be at war with that agency instead. He gave orders to SD-6 agent/grad student Sidney Bristow (Jennifer Garner) and her father Jack Bristow (Victor Garber), both of whom were secretly CIA double agents, except that . . . well, you get the picture.

14
Spin-Offs That Spun Out

A lot of factors go into making a hit series. One of the most important may be the characters. If they mesh and work well together, you're one step closer to the top of the ratings. But when producers have a hit, they don't stop there—naturally, they want another one. They've already got a handful of beloved characters, so what's to stop them from taking one or two for a new show? Sometimes it works, as when *The Jeffersons* left *All in the Family* or when *Frasier* moved on from *Cheers*. But sometimes it doesn't.

1. **AFTERMASH**

When the last episode of *M*A*S*H* appeared in 1983, it set a record for most viewers ever of a single series episode (more than one hundred million). CBS, the network that had broadcast the show for eleven years, knew it was losing a cash cow. Unless . . . what if some of the characters continued? The Korean War was over, so they would have to move back to the United States. It might have been a good idea if we'd followed Hawkeye, Hot Lips, B.J., or even Charles Emerson Winchester. But, no, *AfterMASH* gave us Colonel Potter, Klinger, and Father Mulcahy in a veterans hospital in Missouri. Viewers tentatively tuned in but, quickly realizing that the show was about as imaginative as its stale title, didn't stay long.

2. *JOANIE LOVES CHACHI*

By 1982 we had seen Joanie Cunningham (Erin Moran) grow up over the previous eight years of *Happy Days,* and we had seen her feelings grow for Chachi (Scott Baio), a younger knock-off of his cousin Fonzie (Henry Winkler). But why would we want to see the two of them move from Milwaukee to Chicago so Chachi could follow his dream of becoming a teen singing idol? Answer: We wouldn't. It all turned out OK, though, as Joanie and Chachi soon returned to Milwaukee and their parent TV show with their tails between their legs.

3. *FISH*

In a workplace comedy such as, say, *Barney Miller,* the comedy is based on the characters and situations of the workplace—in the case of *Barney Miller,* the police precinct house. But a hit sitcom is a hit sitcom, and producers and network executives are always looking to capitalize. So in 1977 the elderly Detective Phil Fish (Abe Vigoda) and his wife, Bernice (Florence Stanley), an occasional visitor to the station, bought a big old house and became foster parents of a racially mixed group of five troubled kids. Troubled is right—one was portrayed by *Diff'rent Strokes'* Todd Bridges.

4. *GRADY*

Playing the part of the best friend in a hit series can be a stepping-stone to getting your own series. Such was the case for Whitman Mayo, who played Grady Wilson. Grady moved away from the *Sanford and Son* junkyard in Watts in 1975 to live with his daughter and her family in a middle-class L.A. neighborhood. The move wasn't terribly successful, however, and Grady was quickly back (without his daughter's family) at the junkyard.

5. *THE SANFORD ARMS*

Sanford and Son ended suddenly in 1977 when its stars, Redd Foxx and Demond Wilson, were no longer available to appear in the series. Not to worry—it was quickly explained that Fred and Lamont had moved to Arizona, so the action shifted to the rooming house run by Aunt Esther, Fred's sister-in-law. Grady was here, too, and fortunately wasn't forced to move back in with his daughter. Without Foxx and Wilson, however, the audience wasn't interested, and *The Sanford Arms* lasted only a month.

6. *CHECKING IN*

Maybe spin-offs set in hotels just aren't a good idea. Florence Johnston, *The Jeffersons'* smart-mouthed maid (played by Marla Gibbs), left their employ in 1981 to join the staff of the St. Frederick, an exclusive Manhattan hotel. She must have decided that being a housemaid wasn't so bad, however. When *Checking In* was canceled in less than a month, Florence was right back with George and Weezie.

7. *THE ROPERS*

After only two years as the landlord and landlady to Jack, Janet, and Chrissie on *Three's Company,* Stanley and Helen Roper (Norman Fell and Audra Lindley) had had enough and decided to move up in the world. In 1979 they sold their apartment building and struck out on their own to buy a condo in the more upscale neighborhood of Cheviot Hills. Helen remained a social climber, and Stanley remained rude and common, but without

Jack Tripper to play the foil, the magic just wasn't there.

8. *BEVERLY HILLS BUNTZ*

On the last episode of *Hill Street Blues* in 1987, crass police Lt. Norman Buntz (Dennis Franz) lost his temper (a common occurrence) and punched out the chief of police. He obviously couldn't stay in the unnamed city where that show was set, so what choice did he have? Along with Sid the Snitch, Buntz's *Hill Street Blues* informer, Buntz moved to Beverly Hills to set up his own private detective agency. This fish didn't stay out of water for long, however, as *Beverly Hills Buntz* disappeared after only a few episodes.

9. *SONS OF THUNDER*

Trent and Carlos, the Sons of Thunder, first started making noise on *Walker, Texas Ranger*. After a year of being costars in 1999, Trent (Jimmy Wlcek), a former karate student of Walker's, and police detective Carlos (Marco Sanchez) decided to strike out on their own. In true Norman Buntz tradition, Carlos quit the force to open a detective agency with Trent called Thunder Investigations. Perhaps he should have kept his day job—*Sons of Thunder* lasted only six episodes.

10. *THE TORTELLIS*

From time to time, *Cheers* waitress Carla (Rhea Perlman) received visits from her ex-husband (and father of six of her children), Nick Tortelli (Dan Hedaya). Nick had remarried to tall, blond airhead Loretta (Jean Kasem), but that marriage was on the rocks, as well. When Loretta took off for Las Vegas in 1987 to pursue a showbiz career, Nick followed to keep the marriage together. In Las Vegas, unfortunately, nobody—including the audience—knew his name.

15
Before They Were Stars

Although it can and has happened for a performer to achieve almost instant success in the various fields of entertainment, it's highly unusual. Most entertainers have to travel a long road before they experience enough success that they can support themselves strictly by performing. A classic job for aspiring actors is waiting tables—it provides some flexibility in their schedules so they can go to auditions, and they need little experience to be hired. But working in a restaurant isn't the only occupation TV performers have worked before getting their big break. Here are some career pit stops a few people have taken along the way.

1. **PERRY COMO—BARBER**

Growing up in Canonsburg, Pennsylvania, Perry Como apprenticed as a barber before opening his own barbershop for the coal miners in the town. It was his custom to sing while cutting hair, and he also kept a guitar close by. He was happy with the life he had, but when his friends encouraged him to audition as a professional singer, he did it as a lark. He was as surprised as anyone when he was asked to join the band, which ultimately led to his presence on TV for almost twenty years during the forties, fifties, and sixties.

2. MIKE WALLACE—ACTOR AND GAME SHOW HOST

Known as a ferocious interviewer on *60 Minutes,* Mike Wallace has held down a number of different jobs in broadcasting. He started on radio in Chicago and moved into TV there. As an actor he appeared as Lt. Anthony Kidd in *Stand by for Crime* in 1949 (he was credited as Myron Wallace) as well as in episodes of *Studio One* and *Suspense.* He also worked on game shows throughout the 1950s, hosting *Guess Again, Who's the Boss?, The Big Surprise,* and *Who Pays?,* as well as appearing as a celebrity panelist on *What's in a Word?*

3. BOB DENVER—TEACHER

Some actors become so identified with one or two roles that they become typecast; producers are afraid that audiences will not believe them in any other role. Bob Denver experienced that, first as beatnik and prototype slacker Maynard G. Krebs in *The Many Loves of Dobie Gillis,* and then as the clumsy, not-too-bright Gilligan on *Gilligan's Island.* Before he became a professional actor, Denver earned a degree in political science from Loyola University in Los Angeles and was a teacher in Pacific Palisades, California, during the late 1950s.

4. RICHARD KARN—APARTMENT BUILDING SUPER

Even when a TV job does come along, actors don't know whether the series will be successful. The saying "Don't quit your day job" can be good advice. Richard Karn, who played Al Borland, Tim Taylor's (played by Tim Allen) assistant on *Home Improvement,* had been working as the super in the apartment building where he lived. After *Home Improvement* hit the air, Karn held on to that job for the first year. He has said he was sometimes called to an apartment for repairs just so the residents could show their friends that Al from *Home Improvement* fixed the pipes under their sink.

5. PHIL HARTMAN—GRAPHIC DESIGNER

Before he started to make people laugh in the eighties and nineties on *Saturday Night Live* and

NewsRadio, Phil Hartman had a successful career in design. His work appeared on several album covers for groups such as Poco, America, and others. He also designed a logo for Crosby, Stills, and Nash. Despite the level of accomplishment he had achieved, Hartman found himself bored as a graphic artist, so he enrolled in comedy and improvisational classes with the Groundlings in Los Angeles, which led to an entirely new career.

6. DIANE SAWYER—AMERICA'S JUNIOR MISS

In the early sixties, women didn't have the same career options that they have today, so they got a handhold into a career using more creative methods. One sure way for young girls to get noticed in those days was through beauty pageants. That's exactly what Diane Sawyer did in 1963, first as Kentucky's Junior Miss and then winning the America's Junior Miss crown. Sawyer graduated from Wellesley and took a job in local news in Louisville, Kentucky. Before she got her first job at the network level, Sawyer worked in a number of different positions in the administration of Richard Nixon.

7. GENE RODDENBERRY—POLICE OFFICER

Before Gene Roddenberry broke into television as a writer, and long before he created *Star Trek,* he joined the Los Angeles Police Department, where he became a speechwriter for Chief Bill Parker. Trying to get TV work while on the force, Rodden-berry went to his first writer's meeting with Four Star Productions, where he was quite animated in describing his ideas. During the meeting he felt re-laxed enough to take off his sports coat. After-ward, Roddenberry was quite impressed with how the producers had paid rapt attention to him as he spoke. It was only later that he realized he had gone straight to the meeting from work and was still wearing his shoulder holster in plain sight.

8. JACKIE GLEASON—STUNT DIVER

Many of the pioneers of TV started their entertain-ment careers when there were very few rules. Per-formers had to make their living any way they could, and most of those who later became suc-cessful did whatever would help them get ahead. Although Jackie Gleason was not exactly svelte, he worked for a time as a stunt and high diver at Steel Pier in Atlantic City. He received nineteen dollars a week for diving seventy-five feet outdoors and sixty-five feet indoors. He also made some money working as a pick-up boxer, making two dollars for four rounds—five dollars if he won.

9. BOB HOPE—BOXER

Another comic with some fighting in his back-ground was Bob Hope. He had previously had some dance lessons, which may have come in handy when he fought for a little while under the name Packy East. Later in his career he downplayed the experience, claiming that some of his fans began to call him Rembrandt instead of Packy East, because he spent so much time facing the canvas. He said that he finally gave up fighting altogether when he "was not only being carried out of the ring, but into the ring."

10. DR. RUTH—SNIPER

Television sex expert Dr. Ruth Westheimer has led a very full life. Born in Frankfurt, Germany, she was ten years old when her parents sent her to school in Switzerland for what they all expected would be only a few months until the German persecution of Jews blew over. She spent the entirety of World War II there and never saw her family again. After the war she emigrated to Palestine, where she was trained as a sniper for the Jewish underground. Although Dr. Ruth points out that she never killed anyone, on her twentieth birthday she was wounded by shrapnel from a bomb, from which she fully recovered.

16
Behind-the-Scenes Relationships

Part of what keeps an audience coming back to a series week in and week out is the relationships between the characters. The genuine love and respect or hate and conflict the audience feels emanating from the screen has a tremendous appeal and keeps viewers hooked. The production team and the actors work very hard, of course, to convey these relationships and to make them real. Sometimes they work harder than others. Not every cast and crew gels as firmly behind the scenes as they seem to in front of the camera.

1. VIVIAN VANCE AND WILLIAM FRAWLEY

Viewers would never know it from watching their performances as Fred and Ethel Mertz on *I Love Lucy,* but Vivian Vance and William Frawley had a very tense relationship when they were off camera. Vance felt that Frawley was far too old to be believable as her husband, commenting when she first met him that he should play her father. Frawley returned the sentiments, calling Vance a variety of names behind her back and to her face. Fred and Ethel used to bicker quite a bit, but they always seemed to have an undercurrent of love. The only part that carried over to real life was the bickering.

2. WILLIAM SHATNER AND THE CAST OF STAR TREK

Not every lackluster behind-the-scenes relationship is the result of malice. In the case of *Star Trek*, much of the cast felt that William Shatner, who played Captain James T. Kirk, was distant and uninterested, but Shatner never realized it. The situation was a mystery to him until he began to work on his memoir, *Star Trek Memories*. He thought it would be a good idea to go back and talk to fellow cast members to reminisce about the sixties-era show and movies from the seventies and eighties. Nichelle Nichols, who played Lieutenant Uhuru, laid her cards on the table to let Shatner know how she and her costars felt. Shatner was completely taken aback by the revelation and wanted to strengthen his bonds with his fellow cast members. He wrote: "I was now at a loss in attempting to understand how more than twenty-five years' worth of shared experiences never quite translated into stronger friendships," as though he never realized that they should have. George Takei (Hikaru Sulu) and Walter Koenig (Pavel Chekov) met with him to share old times, but James Doohan (Chief Engineer Montgomery "Scotty" Scott) adamantly refused to see him at all.

3. **ANDY KAUFMAN AS THE HOST OF** *FRIDAYS*

The career of Andy Kaufman has been shrouded in mystery. Kaufman was a comedian, but he worked in a very strange corner of the field. His humor was far from obvious, and those immediately around him often took the brunt of it. One Kaufman event that swirled in rumors for years occurred on February 20, 1981, when he was the guest host of *Fridays,* ABC's late-night clone of *Saturday Night Live* (except that it aired on Friday nights). At the beginning of the show, Kaufman warned the audience that he was going to ignore the script, a very dangerous thing to do on a live broadcast. In the final sketch, Kaufman stopped in the middle, complaining that he felt stupid. The other actors on stage with him—Michael Richards, who later gained fame as Kramer on *Seinfeld,* Melanie Chartoff, and Maryedith Burrell—became understandably upset, and Kaufman threw a glass of water on Richards. The scuffle grew, and soon crewmembers became involved. The obvious question was whether the whole thing had been staged. But as was usually the case with Kaufman, the answer wasn't as obvious. Speculation raged on both sides. It was only many years later that Richards admitted he'd been in on the gag, as had a handful of the behind-the-scenes crew. But Richards's costars on stage had not been aware that sabotage had been planned.

4. JACKIE GLEASON AND THE HONEYMOONERS

His nickname (one that he awarded himself) was "The Great One," and Jackie Gleason has been remembered as one of TV's great comedic geniuses. But not everything was happy backstage at his various TV shows throughout the fifties and sixties. There were a number of reasons for tension, but one of the most noticeable was that since Gleason thought his performance should be fresh, he refused to rehearse. Many TV stars don't get that choice, but Gleason had enough power on his show that he could get away with it. His costars, particularly Audrey Meadows (Alice) and Art Carney (Ed Norton), had to rehearse their scenes without him. The performers could never be sure what Gleason would do on stage, and the process became nerve-racking. Meadows has said Gleason often brought her to tears. As they were ready to go before the cameras together as Ralph and Alice Kramden, she would tell him, "You are simply a dreadful man."

5.   CARROLL O'CONNOR AND NORMAN LEAR

Artistically, the partnership of Carroll O'Connor and Norman Lear on *All in the Family* changed television forever. But life was not always so smooth behind the scenes. As the producer, Lear ran the show, but O'Connor was always quite assertive in offering his opinion, sometimes too much so. Lear at times considered ways to get O'Connor off the series, a move that seems quite ill considered with twenty-twenty hindsight. Although their differences were worked out to the point that they could continue to do the show for more than a decade, from 1971 to 1983, and O'Connor even confessed that he had sometimes been nastier than he had needed to be, the hard feelings remained. In the nineties O'Connor wanted to bring back the character of Archie Bunker, but Lear believed that this would be a bad idea. A photo shoot for *Vanity Fair* magazine reunited several actors from various Norman Lear series, but O'Connor was conspicuous in his absence.

6.   SHELLEY LONG AND THE CAST OF *CHEERS*

Another set that wasn't entirely happy was that of *Cheers*. Most of the cast got along together very well, but Shelley Long, who played intellectual barmaid Diane Chambers, never quite fit in. On-screen Diane was a fish out of water at the Boston bar, often at odds with the other characters, and that situation was echoed in real life as well. Long was often blamed for delays in taping because of the length of time she took to change costume. As the show progressed, the writers made an effort to tell stories that took place in just one day so she'd have no need to change. Long's original dressing room had been on a different floor than the sound-stage, but a new area was built for her nearby so she wouldn't have far to go between scenes. She and Ted Danson, who played Sam Malone, the bar owner and Diane's sometime romantic interest, particularly didn't get along—yelling matches between the two could be heard backstage from time to time. When Long left the show in 1987, her castmates weren't sorry to see her go.

7.   DAVID CARUSO AND THE CAST AND CREW OF *NYPD BLUE*

A performer who shone very brightly but very briefly was David Caruso as Detective John Kelly, a founding cast member on *NYPD Blue* in 1993.

The show was about the detective team of Kelly and Andy Sipowicz, played by Dennis Franz, but Sipowicz was gunned down in the first episode, so Kelly got most of the spotlight as his partner recovered. Although Caruso's intense style made for very compelling television, it led to turmoil and even tantrums on the set. One story relates how Caruso kicked a wastebasket toward Franz and then walked off the set. Before the end of the season, Franz was no longer talking to Caruso. When Caruso wanted a raise and an adjusted work schedule to star in movies, producers Steven Bochco and David Milch were not able to come to terms with him, and he left the show after a few episodes in the second season, to be replaced by Jimmy Smits. Caruso asserted that he wasn't actually having tantrums; his yelling was simply an attempt to keep himself psyched toward the end of a long workday. Bochco flatly stated that he would never work with Caruso again. The cast and crew probably weren't shattered when Caruso's movie career flopped almost immediately.

8. CYBILL SHEPHERD AND BRUCE WILLIS/ CYBILL SHEPHERD AND CHRISTINE BARANSKI

Cybill Shepherd has had difficult relationships with her costars on two different series from 1985 until

1998. On *Moonlighting* she and Bruce Willis
played partners in a detective agency. Despite a
potential closeness (Shepherd and Willis almost
became intimate on one occasion, but each
thought the better of it), the costars developed
more and more conflict as the show grew in popularity. *Moonlighting*'s producer and creator Glenn
Gordon Caron also took part in the fray and ultimately left the series as a result.

Many observers saw a similar situation develop
on the set of *Cybill,* Shepherd's late-nineties situation comedy. She played Cybill Sheridan, a
middle-aged Hollywood actress, and Christine
Baranski was her best friend, Maryann Thorpe. As
on *Moonlighting,* Shepherd was the name star
costarring with a relative unknown. Although there
weren't dramatic blow-ups, the relationship was
very tense. As the new face, Baranski received a
lot of attention, winning an Emmy in her first year.
There were other troubles backstage, and more
than a few writers and producers came and went.
By the time the series ended its fourth season, the
decision to cancel hadn't been made by CBS, but
the expectation was overwhelming. On what
turned out to be the final episode, Baranski didn't
even stay until the end of filming. After finishing
her scenes, she left the set without saying goodbye.

9. PENNY MARSHALL AND CINDY WILLIAMS

Happy Days is one show that is renowned for the happiness and calm behind its scenes. No one was jealous when an unknown Henry Winkler rose to a starring part as the Fonz. Into that pleasant environment in 1975 stepped Penny Marshall and Cindy Williams as Laverne and Shirley, ready for a double date with Richie and Fonzie. That date was so successful that *Laverne & Shirley* was quickly picked up as a series, and it hit number one in the ratings on its very first episode.

Unfortunately, the atmosphere on the set of *Laverne & Shirley* was the exact opposite of *Happy Days*. Penny Marshall's brother Garry produced *Happy Days* and had the same responsibilities on *Laverne & Shirley*. He was unable to keep writers or producers on the series for a full season. Conflict also arose between the two stars, who had been writing partners before they appeared on *Happy Days*. Williams was concerned that Penny Marshall would receive special treatment because she was the producer's sister. Penny Marshall was afraid that Garry would overcompensate for that fact and give Williams special treatment. Toward the end of the series, Williams got married and became pregnant. When she wasn't able to work out a schedule with the studio to allow for time with her new family, she left the show.

10. THE CAST OF *FRASIER* AND EDDIE THE DOG

Sure, the dog on *Frasier* was cute, but he stole many of the scenes he was in, and the cast of that successful sitcom had no patience for him. Eddie the dog was played by Moose, a Jack Russell terrier. Moose generally remained aloof from the rest of the cast, preferring to stay in his own office during the breaks in taping. After finding success on *Frasier* in 1993, Moose took on the whole star trip. When he flew, Moose always went first class, and he didn't have to sit in one of those travel cages, either. John Mahoney, who played Frasier Crane's father, Martin, the longtime owner of Eddie, said that if he passed Moose on the street, Moose would be unlikely to recognize him. He pointed out that Moose was more actor than dog. The dog was so heavily trained that the normal reflexes one would expect from him were not present. His costars complained that he expressed very little affection and didn't particularly enjoy being petted. In the ultimate indignity, Moose's costars sometimes had to spread liver paste on their faces when Eddie was supposed to lick them during the show. But, as always with TV, it was what was on the screen that counted, and Moose's portrayal of Eddie was gold. If the viewers loved him, what did it matter what went on behind the scenes?

17
Prime-Time Cartoons

Cartoons have been a part of television since its earliest days, although they have primarily been targeted to children and broadcast on weekday afternoons and Saturday mornings. The producers of the cartoons, however, probably believed that at least a handful of adults were peeking in as well. From time to time, therefore, they would make animated series intended for a mixed audience of children and adults, or sometimes even adults alone. Here are a few series that have escaped the ghetto of children's programming for the oasis of prime time.

1. *THE FLINTSTONES*

The first animated series made exclusively for nighttime viewing, *The Flintstones* was also the first prime-time animated show to become a hit. Produced by the animation team of William Hanna and Joseph Barbera, it first hit the air in 1960 and stayed there for six years. Others have noted that *The Flintstones* had more than a passing similarity to *The Honeymooners,* a fact that cannot be denied, but the show's animation allowed for a greater variety of situations and locations than *The Honeymooners,* who were primarily limited to Ralph Kramden's apartment.

The success of *The Flintstones* inspired Hanna-Barbera to create more cartoons for prime time. *Top Cat* echoed *The Phil Silvers Show* (replacing Sergeant Bilko and his men with alley cats living in New York), even to the point of having Maurice Gosfield perform the voice of Benny the Ball, who corresponded to Private Duane Doberman, his character on the previous program. *The Jetsons* essentially borrowed the family from the newspaper comic strip *Blondie* (which had also appeared in movies and a TV series) and placed them in the distant future. Penny Singleton, who had played the part of Blondie in a series of movies, was the voice of Jane Jetson.

2. *CALVIN & THE COLONEL*

Taking its cue from *The Flintstones, Calvin & the Colonel* was completely appropriated from a successful radio (and less successful TV) series, re-visiting the characters from *Amos & Andy*. The brainchild of Freeman Gosden and Charles Correll, the white performers who played them on the radio, *Amos & Andy* was a full-fledged sensation during the thirties. Jack Benny remembered movie theaters promising to turn off the movie and turn on the radio when the show was on.

The title characters were African American men from the South who relocated to Chicago, where they got involved in various shenanigans, usually at the behest of Kingfish, the head of their local lodge. In later years, however, the series came to be considered racist. Due partially to efforts by the NAACP, the television show, which featured an all African American cast, was canceled in 1953. Eight years later, however, Gosden and Correll resurrected their concept, avoiding the racial baggage by using funny animals. Calvin Burnside, a bear, replaced Andy, and Colonel Montgomery J. Klaxon, a fox, stood in for Kingfish. Gosden and Correll themselves provided voices. The animation wasn't terribly good, however, and the show lasted only a year in prime time. (Reruns continued on Saturday mornings.)

3. *THE BULLWINKLE SHOW*

Moving from weekday afternoons to evenings in 1961 were Rocky the flying squirrel and his best

In 1961, Rocket J. Squirrel and Bullwinkle J. Moose rose above their origins in daytime TV to spend a year on the NBC prime-time schedule. The name of the cartoon show, originally *Rocky and His Friends* on ABC, was changed to *The Bullwinkle Show* when it jumped networks.

friend, Bullwinkle J. Moose. Titled *Rocky and His Friends* when it aired in the afternoon, the name was changed to *The Bullwinkle Show* for prime time. The show was produced by Jay Ward, a former real estate broker who entered the field of animation when his friend Alexander Anderson asked for a loan to produce *Crusader Rabbit,* the first cartoon made for television. Rather than just lending the money, Ward became involved in all aspects of the production.

The Bullwinkle Show may have had the most sophisticated writing of any animated show in the early sixties, with many of the jokes shooting right over the heads of children on the way to their actual target, parents and other adults. Rocky and Bullwinkle's nemeses were foreign agents Boris Badenov and Natasha Fatale. Also appearing on the show were cartoons featuring the brilliant time-traveling dog, Mr. Peabody, and his boy, Sherman, and "Fractured Fairy Tales," in which Edward Everett Horton narrated well-known fairy tales with a modern, and often cynical, twist.

4. THE ALVIN SHOW

By the time Alvin and his chipmunk brothers got their own series in 1961, they had already been stars for a few years. Their first appearance in any medium was on the Christmas novelty record "The Chipmunk Song," a favorite of baby boomers everywhere. That song hit number one during the 1958 Christmas season, and it was soon followed by more singles and albums. Songwriter and performer Ross Bagdasarian sang all the parts, speeding up the tape to create the voices of the chipmunk trio.

In that first record, he had also established the personalities of Alvin, the youngest and most rambunctious of the chipmunks, and David Seville, their human guardian, so it wasn't much of a jump to establish Dave, Alvin, and Alvin's brothers Simon and Theodore, in their own animated show. Again, Bagdasarian, with his tape-speed tricks, provided all the voices. The series lasted just a year in prime time but continued for several years in Saturday morning reruns. In 1983, Ross Bagdasarian Jr. brought Dave and the chipmunks back for a new round of Saturday morning episodes.

5. *BEANY AND CECIL*

When *Matty's Funday Funnies* started out in 1960, it was mostly a dumping ground for older theatrical cartoons such as *Casper, the Friendly Ghost* and *Little Audrey*. Before too long, however, it shifted over to the adventures of a boy and his best friend, a sea serpent. The characters started out as puppets in a local Los Angeles kids' show by former Warner Brothers animator Bob Clampett, but they found more successful life in cartoon form. Shortly after they began appearing on *Matty's Funday Funnies,* the show was renamed *Beany and Cecil.* The cartoons were full of wit, intelligence, irreverence, and bad puns. Legend has it that they even counted luminaries such as Groucho Marx and Albert Einstein among their fans. Beany traveled with his uncle, Captain Horatio K. Huffenpuff, on the *Leakin' Lena,* and Cecil the Sea-Sick Sea Serpent was never far away. Together they ran into a variety of characters, such as their primary villain, Dishonest John, and Tear-a-long the Dotted Lion.

6. *JONNY QUEST*

Although no animated series of the early sixties besides *The Flintstones* gained any lasting measure of prime-time success, Hanna-Barbera still had a couple of tricks up their sleeve. In the fall of 1964, that animation studio debuted an adventure show. No more goofy characters like Fred Flintstone or George Jetson. No more funny animals echoing established sitcoms. *Jonny Quest,* created by cartoonist Doug Wildey, depicted the young son of world-renowned scientist Dr. Benton Quest and the exciting and exotic international exploits they shared with pilot, tutor, and bodyguard Race Bannon, young East Indian friend Hadji, and their dog, Bandit. This thrilling half hour was unlike any cartoon that had been shown on television, combining foreign intrigue, mystery, and suspense. Young Jonny lived a life that was the envy of every kid watching.

7. *WHERE'S HUDDLES*

Ten years after the premiere of *The Flintstones,* Hanna-Barbera brought their last prime-time cartoon show to air. *Where's Huddles* was about two pals who played professional football for the Rhinos. Ed Huddles was the quarterback, and his best friend, Bubba McCoy, was the center. Their relationship was a virtual replay of that between Fred Flintstone and Barney Rubble, and that wasn't the only echo of *The Flintstones*. Mel Blanc, who provided Barney's voice, also lent his voice to Bubba, and Jean Vander Pyl, the voice of Wilma Flintstone, was heard again as Ed Huddles's wife, Marge. Even Alan Reid, the voice of Fred, was back—this time as Rhinos coach Mad Dog Maloney. But after *Where's Huddles* it was back to Saturday morning for cartoon shows. There would not be another one in prime time for almost twenty years.

8. *THE SIMPSONS*

As if on cue, almost twenty years later in December 1989, Fox Television started to air half-hour episodes of *The Simpsons*. Like *The Flintstones* almost thirty years earlier, *The Simpsons* blazed the trail of animation in prime time. The characters in *The Simpsons* had already appeared on TV for a couple of years—in animated shorts for *The Tracey Ullman Show*. They were the brainchild of cartoonist Matt Groening, who claimed he took the family's names—though he insists not their personalities—from his own father, Homer; mother, Marge; and sisters, Lisa and Maggie. The name "Bart" is simply *Brat* with the two middle letters switched.

The humor was oriented very much toward adults, and although the quality varied somewhat from season to season, the show remained fresh and funny for years on end. In fact, *The Simpsons* was far more successful than anyone had ever expected. Unlike series that featured live actors, *The Simpsons* was able to keep its characters, including the kids, at the same age indefinitely. This led to an intriguing paradox: The series itself remained in production long enough that it grew older than its star, ten-year-old Bart.

9. *KING OF THE HILL*

After gaining notoriety with MTV's animated couch-potato music video fans *Beavis and Butt-head,* Mike Judge moved away from cable to the larger audiences of network TV. With Greg Daniels, a former writer and producer for *The Simpsons,* in 1997 Judge took aim at the center of Middle America. They created Hank Hill and his family and friends in Arlen, Texas, a suburb of Houston. Hank was a normal middle-aged father with a little bit of redneck stereotype tossed in for good measure. He was a propane salesman who tried to maintain himself as head of his own household, which included his wife, Peggy, a no-nonsense substitute teacher who wouldn't let Hank get away with anything; his son, Bobby, who disappointed Hank with his disinterest in football and other traditional Texas pastimes; and his niece, Louanne, who left beauty school to enter junior college. Although *King of the Hill* didn't take advantage of animation to portray situations that would be too difficult for live actors—it could easily have been a regular sitcom—the writing was sharp and funny, and the show deserved the audience and success it achieved.

10. *SOUTH PARK*

Set in the town of South Park, Colorado, *South Park* featured four elementary-school boys: Stan was the most normal of the characters, but that wasn't saying much; Eric Cartman filled the role of the stereotypical fat, stupid one; Kyle was the smart one; and Kenny was the younger tagalong kid who was killed in almost every episode of the first five seasons (to which Stan inevitably responded: "Oh my God, they killed Kenny!").

The show was among the most irreverent television series ever, depicting the boys' interactions with God and Jesus, various pop culture icons, and aliens and monsters. The animation was intentionally crude, as the show came out of a video Christmas card by animators Matt Stone and Trey Parker that animated small construction-paper cutouts. That effect, computerized for the actual series, was retained. The Christmas card quickly made the rounds of Hollywood, picking up George Clooney as an early champion, and resulted in this Comedy Central cable series by Stone and Parker. For his early support, the creators invited Clooney to act as the voice of Sparky, Stan's gay dog. Sparky never spoke (he was a dog, after all), but Clooney provided all of his barks.

18
Here Today, Gone Tomorrow

People who know their TV history are well aware of the longest-lasting TV series. *Meet the Press* has been on the air for more than half a century following its debut in 1947, and *The Tonight Show* is well into middle age itself. In prime time, there's *60 Minutes,* which has been broadcast continuously since 1968. The dramatic series that ran the longest was *Gunsmoke,* at twenty seasons. But what of those series that come and go, that barely see the light of day? These are some shows that network executives couldn't cancel fast enough.

1. **YOU'RE IN THE PICTURE**

This 1961 game show hosted by Jackie Gleason is legendary in its awfulness. The concept was that celebrities would stick their heads through holes in a picture and guess what was in the picture. On most celebrity game shows, the panelists take turns asking a question, making a guess, or doing whatever the show required. Not here. Everyone talked over everyone else, so no one could be heard clearly, Gleason had trouble keeping order, and everyone involved was embarrassed the next morning. Instead of putting themselves through another week, Gleason took the stage alone for what would have been the second episode and filled the half hour with a sheepish apology. "*You're in the Picture* laid, without a doubt, the biggest bomb," he said, getting straight to the point. "I've seen bombs in my day, but this would make the H-bomb look like a two-inch salute." *You're in the Picture* never reappeared. The time slot was filled instead by *The Jackie Gleason Show,* in which Gleason held a casual one-on-one interview with a different guest each week.

2. *TURN-ON*

Another notorious turkey, *Turn-On* came from George Schlatter, at the time in the midst of a huge success as producer of *Rowan & Martin's Laugh-In*. A half-hour comedy show on ABC that was ostensibly programmed by computer (when that was still a novel idea) but had actually been in development for more than a year, *Turn-On* was supposed to out-*Laugh-In* *Laugh-In*. It took *Laugh-In*'s quick-cut formula and amped it up until some bits were only a few seconds long. Unfortunately, it may have been fast, but it wasn't funny. *Turn-On* was, however, quite risqué by the standards of 1969. During the show, which aired on February 5, TV-station switchboards across the country lit up with complaints. Tim Conway, the guest star for the first and only show (does that make him a regular?) has claimed the show was canceled before that episode even finished airing, but this is likely an exaggeration. Although cancellation may have been a fait accompli by the end of the half hour, the official decision was still a couple of days in coming.

3. *CO-ED FEVER*

Anyone who has watched TV for any length of time knows that it's a copycat medium. If something is a hit, everyone else will be jumping on the bandwagon in no time. That was certainly the case when *National Lampoon's Animal House* hit it big in the movie theaters during the summer of 1978. By 1979, all three networks had developed a wacky fraternity or college sitcom. None of these were successful, but CBS had the biggest flop. *Co-Ed Fever,* featuring David Keith as a student living in a girls' dorm that had recently gone coed, was scheduled for a Monday time slot, but it was given a "special preview" on Sunday night. On February 4 CBS aired *Co-Ed Fever*'s one and only episode. It was such a disappointment that it never made it to its scheduled Monday nighttime period.

4. *MELBA*

Although she won a Tony Award for her work on Broadway and got on the record charts as a singer, Melba Moore's TV career was not quite as stellar. The premise of her sitcom, *Melba,* didn't seem to be out of the ordinary—she was a single mother with a daughter, and she worked at the Manhattan Visitors' Center in New York. What was out of the ordinary was its public reception. Almost nobody watched. Gone after one episode in January 1986, the show had a few more episodes already completed. Late in the summer of that year, CBS was so desperate for programming to fill its schedule before the new fall season that it brought *Melba* back for a few weeks. Its first comeback episode on August 2 was part of the lowest-rated evening of television CBS had ever experienced.

5. *SOUTH OF SUNSET*

Some shows raise higher expectations than others. One with very high expectations was *South of*

Sunset, which starred rock legend Glenn Frey of the Eagles as a down-on-his-luck private eye and was heavily promoted by CBS in the 1993 season. The network had broadcast the World Series that year, which normally provides an excellent outlet for advertising. Frey had already made successful guest appearances on *Miami Vice,* and his own show was the next logical step. Unfortunately, logic had nothing to do with the response to *South of Sunset.* Its premiere had among the lowest—if not the lowest—ratings ever for a fall network premiere, and it never got a second chance to try to raise that number, as it was gone before the second episode aired. Several episodes that had been completed but were never shown on CBS showed up later on MTV during the "Hell Freezes Over" Eagles reunion tour.

6. *THE GREAT DEFENDER*

Essentially a fish-out-of-water comedy, *The Great Defender* may have portrayed a great lawyer, but it was pretty miserable television. Michael Rispoli played Lou Frischetti, the defender of the title, who attracted most of his clientele by advertising on TV. Although his clients were primarily blue collar, Frischetti's style caught the eye of Jason DeWitt (Richard Kiley), the senior partner of a prestigious Boston firm, who asked him to join in the hopes of

shaking up his associates, particularly his grandson. Whether his plan was successful will always
remain a mystery, as the series was pulled after
the one episode in March 1995. Fox found itself in
the same situation as CBS had a few years earlier,
with a hole in its summer schedule, so a few more
episodes of the already-canceled series saw the
light of day.

7. *PUBLIC MORALS*

Steven Bochco has been one of the most successful producers in television history. He can count
among his triumphs such groundbreaking series
as *Hill Street Blues, L.A. Law,* and *NYPD Blue.* He
is such a prolific producer (he has well over a
dozen series to his name) that he's bound to come
up with a stinker every now and again. *Public Morals* may be his most infamous. A sitcom revolving
around a New York City vice squad who spent
much of their time pursuing prostitutes, the show
was under fire before it ever hit the air. Bochco initially claimed to be pushing the envelope of what
was acceptable on television with the show's crude
language and situations, but he finally gave in and
toned down the first episode. The network at least
expected people to tune in for the controversy, but
barely anyone did. While CBS may have tried to
work with a high-rated problem series, they had

no patience whatsoever for a low-rated one, and *Public Morals* never showed up again.

8. *LAWLESS*

During the nineties, popular culture had an obsession with football player Brian Bosworth. He was outrageous as a college player in Oklahoma, both on and off the field. The Seattle Seahawks picked him in the first round of the NFL draft and gave him a huge contract. During his first pro season, he wrote his best-selling memoir, *The Boz*. Unfortunately a career-ending injury hit him in only his third year. The obvious place to go was movies and TV, right? It might have been obvious, but it wasn't successful. Bosworth made movies, but each one fared worse than the one before, until his appearances were all straight to video. Somehow, in 1997 Fox still thought it would be a good idea to give Bosworth a show. *Lawless* starred Bosworth as John Lawless, a motorcycle-riding private investigator who left Special Forces because he wanted more excitement. No more people wanted to watch him on TV than wanted to see him in movies, and the ratings on the premiere were an embarrassment—so embarrassing that Fox made sure it was never heard from again.

9. *DOT COMEDY*

America's Funniest Home Videos had been a hit in the nineties, and ABC thought it might be able to repeat that success for the new decade with this show. *Dot Comedy* was based on a British show of the same name and purported to present funny items from the Internet, such as Web pages or e-mails, just as *America's Funniest Home Videos* presented amateur videos from its viewers. Before the debut, an ABC executive said, "*Dot Comedy* is an innovative, daring show that taps in to the immediate, electric nature of the Internet. We couldn't be more thrilled." Hosted by stand-up comedy twins Jason and Randy Sklar along with Annabelle Gurwitch, *Dot Comedy* apparently couldn't find anything immediate, electric, or funny on the Internet, at least not anything that hadn't already been forwarded around the world in e-mail. Apparently the network could have been more thrilled when the dismal ratings from the December 8, 2000, episode started trickling in. They immediately pulled it from the schedule, leaving the viewing public to find Internet laughs on their own.

10. *BUILT TO LAST*

There have been a number of shows that were canceled after two episodes, such as *Aliens in the Family*; *Big Shamus, Little Shamus,* starring Brian Dennehy; or *Wind on Water,* with Bo Derek. But for its name alone, mention must be made of *Built to Last,* which stayed on the air for a full three epi-

sodes in 1997. Although the title refers to the construction firm run by computer programmer
Royale Watkins (played by stand-up comic Royale
Watkins) after his father (Paul Winfield) had a
heart attack, it takes on a special poignance in
light of its short history. Perhaps the show's creators felt that they had a certain amount of protec-
tion with their title, but if so, they should have
realized that they could never successfully appeal
to network programmers' sentimental sides. One
has to wonder if the programmers felt a tinge of
melancholy when they pulled the plug, or if they
experienced a perverse joy at the irony.

19
They're All Wet

The sea—dark, mysterious, and sometimes dangerous—has always had an allure to those of us who spend our lives on the land. From the ancient legend of Jason and the Argonauts to the more recent *Moby-Dick* and *20,000 Leagues Under the Sea,* writers have written about the sea and the listening, reading, and viewing audiences have lapped it up. Television, of course, is not to be left behind by such stories and has its own handful of shows that saw most of their action beneath the waves.

1. *VOYAGE TO THE BOTTOM OF THE SEA*

Following the 1961 film of the same name that starred Walter Pidgeon and Peter Lorre, *Voyage to the Bottom of the Sea* chronicled the adventures of the crew of the atomic submarine *Seaview*. Irwin Allen had written, produced, and directed the film, and he was in charge of its TV incarnation as well. Richard Basehart took over the role of Admiral Harrison Nelson, a scientific genius who designed the sub and operated out of his own Nelson Institute of Marine Research. Although Admiral Nelson was ultimately in charge, the day-to-day running of the ship was left to Captain Lee Crane (David Hedison).

An atomic sub was advanced technology in the early sixties, so this show tended toward science fiction, as the *Seaview* ran into more than its fair share of sea monsters. The special effects were actually quite good for the time, but they don't stand up today. In that unfortunate detail as well as many others, 1964's *Voyage to the Bottom of the Sea* set the tone of all Allen's TV work to follow. He later had success with *Lost in Space, The Time Tunnel,* and *Land of the Giants*. Irwin Allen later returned to film with *The Poseidon Adventure,* which sparked the disaster movie trend of the seventies.

2. *MAN FROM ATLANTIS*

Taking an even more fantastic point of view was *Man from Atlantis*. Patrick Duffy played Mark Harris, a man, as the title suggests, from the lost continent of Atlantis. He was found washed up on the shore by marine researcher Dr. Elizabeth Merrill (Belinda Montgomery), who nursed him back to health. Maybe it was the webbing between his fingers and toes and the gills he had instead of lungs that tipped her off, but she quickly discovered that Mark was the last surviving Atlantean. He could swim the ocean depths without any equipment, and he had great strength. Naturally, she asked him to join her scientific work at the Foundation for Oceanic Research.

Their undersea adventures, Mark swimming freely while Belinda was usually limited to her submarine, went far beyond normal oceanography as they encountered aliens and beings from other dimensions. Mark's odd swimming style recalled an eel or dolphin: He kept his arms to his sides and, for want of a better term, flapped his body through the water. Although *Man from Atlantis* shot fewer than twenty episodes for the 1977 season, for reasons that are difficult to guess, it was the first American TV series sold for viewing in the People's Republic of China. Patrick Duffy later had great success playing landlubber Bobby Ewing on *Dallas*.

3. ***FLIPPER***

Although *Flipper* didn't have the intricate undersea adventures featured in the two previous series, the only contact the title star made with his costars was when he stuck his head up out of the water. The dolphin Flipper originally appeared in a movie that was also named for him, and that movie had a sequel, *Flipper's New Adventure,* while this series was on the air. In both movies and this series, Luke Halprin played Sandy Hicks, the boy who befriended Flipper. He lived with his younger brother, Bud (Tommy Norden), and their father, Porter (Brian Kelly), the chief ranger of Coral Key Park in Florida. This series, like both of the movies, was produced by Ivan Tors, who built a career out of movies and television shows about wildlife and nature. One of his specialties was underwater action, a fact of which this list takes great advantage— four of the ten shows are Ivan Tors productions. *Flipper* aired for three years in the mid-sixties.

4. *SEA HUNT*

Ivan Tors's first show to take place beneath the waves, *Sea Hunt* was turned down by each of the networks because they didn't believe there was much potential for undersea adventure. Taking the show into syndication in 1957, Tors was stepping into uncharted territory himself, and he wasn't sure how much of the show to actually set underwater. Lloyd Bridges played Mike Nelson, a navy-trained but now freelance frogman, available for all

Lloyd Bridges was ready to take on all comers as freelance frogman Mike Nelson in *Sea Hunt*. As the series progressed, more and more of the action was shot underwater.

your undersea investigation needs. Although that may sound a bit far-fetched, Nelson was hired for a variety of activities. He could salvage stolen material that had been lost at sea; he could take part in rescue operations; he could even thwart undersea crime when he found it.

Although the point of the series was to portray scuba diving, the producers had no idea how much the audience would accept, so they started with about a quarter of each episode spent underwater. Tors later said, "We soon found out that was what the audience wanted—water, water, and more water." The producers soon upped the amount of underwater footage to about half of each episode. *Sea Hunt* went on to become one of the most successful syndicated series TV had ever seen.

5. *THE AQUANAUTS*

Perhaps CBS had second thoughts when they saw the success of *Sea Hunt.* In 1960, three years after that show hit the airwaves, Ivan Tors was onboard with the network for *The Aquanauts*. This series featured two divers, Drake Andrews (Keith Lawson) and Larry Lahr (Jeremy Slate). Their adventures went along swimmingly for a few months until health concerns forced Lawson to drop out of the series. His character rejoined the navy and was replaced with Mike Madison (Ron Ely). In a move that may or may not have been related, the undersea action was curtailed about a month later. Lahr and Madison set up shop on Malibu Beach and began to find diversions on land to keep them busy and out of the water. The name of the show became *Malibu Run* to reflect this change. Even so, it was still canceled at the end of the season. Ron Ely was not yet finished with the sea; nor, perhaps, was it with him. After a successful two years as

Tarzan in the late sixties, Ely returned in 1987 with an updated version of *Sea Hunt*.

6. ***OPERATION NEPTUNE***

Playing mostly to the kids, *Operation Neptune* offered big-time submarine adventure in 1953. When its ships started to disappear, the navy became quite suspicious that it was under attack by an unknown undersea enemy. The navy needed investigative action, so Commander Bill Hollister and his submarine were brought in. Hollister (Todd Griffin) was certainly the right man for the job: He had spent so much time performing underwater research that he'd gained the nickname of "Captain Neptune." Along with his assistant, Dink (Richard Holland), Hollister discovered that the evil Kebeda of Nadiria (Harold Conklin) had designs to destroy all surface dwellers. *Operation Neptune* took the form of a serial, and in its eight half-hour episodes, Hollister and Dink had been captured, had escaped by taking their own prisoner, and had seen their prisoner escape. The full story was never completed, and the last we saw Hollister and Dink, they had become caught in a raging storm at sea.

7. ***FISH POLICE***

Fish Police was an animated half hour with an impressive cast of voices. It presented a hard-boiled detective setup in which the characters were fish or other undersea creatures. Inspector Gil, a detective in Fish City voiced by John Ritter, was the hero, and he was joined by Chief Abalone (Ed Asner); Calamari, the local crime boss (Hector Elizondo); and Sharkster, Calamari's crooked lawyer (Tim Curry).

Maybe there was some potential, but the show's writing and execution were extremely poor. The climax of one episode involved Inspector Gil threatening to push another fish out a window if he didn't provide the information Gil was seeking. Viewers, of course, remembered that all the action took place underwater, so this was no threat at all. Gil got what he was after, but he couldn't help but ridicule the fish who had taken that threat seriously. After all, Gil pointed out, they were all underwater—he was hardly going to fall out the window. When a show depends on its fish characters being so stupid they don't even realize they can swim, it bodes ill. *Fish Police* was hooked and reeled in from the schedule in three weeks.

8. *PRIMUS*

Ivan Tors's final attempt to make a television series about scuba divers, *Primus* starred Robert Brown, who had previously starred as Jason Bolt, the oldest brother on 1968's *Here Come the Brides*.

In what was, unfortunately, *Sea Hunt* warmed over, Carter Primus was an oceanographer for hire, equipped with more hi-tech gadgets than Mike Nelson had, such as *Big Kate,* an underwater robot, and *Pegasus,* a small sub outfitted for underwater photography. *Primus* was a syndicated show in the fall of 1971, but for various reasons the market was flooded with syndicated shows at that time. While fans of *Sea Hunt* may have had their hopes up for a series that could follow in that fine tradition, *Primus* didn't have the writing of its forerunner. Without the spark that separates a great TV show from a run-of-the-mill one, *Primus* wasn't able to stand out in an overcrowded field. It lasted only twenty-two episodes.

9. *THE UNDERSEA WORLD OF JACQUES COUSTEAU*

While he never actually had an official series, world-renowned undersea explorer Jacques Cousteau made scientific documentaries that were featured on television as specials so often that it sure seemed like he did. Cousteau, a French biologist who had developed a romance with the sea, presented his first documentary on American network television on the *Omnibus* program in 1954 and continued making new documentaries for decades. Many of these were shot onboard Cousteau's boat *Calypso,* and they opened the vastness and variety of ocean life wide for American viewers. The specials generally focused on a distinct animal or aspect of undersea life, such as dolphins, sharks, or sea otters.

Cousteau was actually an explorer, and his work often broke new ground in terms of experiencing and understanding different parts of the world. He was one of the first filmmakers to journey to Antarctica, shooting some of the earliest film the general public ever got to see of that frozen continent's ice formations and other natural wonders. He also explored and shot a lot of footage of Australia's Great Barrier Reef. In the eighties and nineties, Cousteau started to focus on the great rivers of the world, exploring in detail the Nile, the Amazon, the Mississippi, and the St. Lawrence. Cousteau remained in the public eye almost until his death in 1997 at the age of eighty-seven.

10. *SEAQUEST DSV*

Steven Spielberg was at the helm of this 1993 undersea drama that returned firmly to the tradition of *Voyage to the Bottom of the Sea.* It was set in the year 2018, with the premise that humans were establishing colonies on the ocean floor. The name of the submarine was *seaQuest,* and *DSV* stood for Deep Submergence Vehicle. The vessel's captain was Nathan Hale Bridger, played by Roy Scheider, who had played the sheriff in Spielberg's *Jaws*. In an echo of *Voyage to the Bottom of the Sea,* Bridger also designed the 1,000-foot craft.

The creative aspects of the show were troubled, however, and the series endured two major shake-ups in its two and a half years on the air. At the end of the first season, the *seaQuest* was destroyed, replaced by a smaller crew and a smaller craft in the new season. A few new characters were introduced to replace some of those who had left. Still not satisfied, however, the producers performed a more extreme act at the end of the second season. For the summer cliffhanger, the craft was taken to another planet and apparently destroyed. The series was renewed, so it turned out the ship hadn't been destroyed; instead it returned to Earth a dozen years later (although the crew had mysteriously not aged), and the show changed its name to *seaQuest 2032*. That still wasn't enough, however, and the submarine disappeared for good in the middle of the season.

20
Try and Try Again

There's no telling what factors mix together to produce a TV star. One of the most important, however, is timing. The performer must be ready, and the audience must be ready for the performer. If the timing is not right on either side, we might see particular performers and pay no attention whatsoever. But under different circumstances, they might shine so much we can't keep our eyes off them. That's why it's so important that TV performers keep putting themselves out there until everything comes together. These are some TV stars who had to wait patiently for that to happen.

1. GEORGE CLOONEY

The classic example of someone having to wait for the right time may be George Clooney. When *ER* stormed the ratings charts, the audience sat up and took notice of Clooney as Dr. Doug Ross. What they likely didn't know was this was someone they had probably seen before in any of a number of parts. Besides shows on which he guest-starred for a week or two, Clooney was a regular on seven different TV series before *ER* came along.

His first show, believe it or not, was a 1984 sitcom called *E/R* with Elliott Gould. Clooney played Ace, a young, hotshot doctor in the emergency room of a Chicago hospital. Others in the cast who went on to bigger things were Mary McDonnell of *Dances with Wolves* and Jason Alexander of *Seinfeld.* Clooney next spent a year on *The Facts of Life,* playing carpenter George Burnett, helping to rebuild Mrs. Garrett's store, which had burned down the previous season. After that he soon showed up as Booker on the first year of *Roseanne* in 1988. Booker was Roseanne's boss and Jackie's sometime boyfriend, and the series rose to number two in the ratings that year.

From there Clooney got what might have looked like his big break: In 1990 he starred in his own series, *Sunset Beat,* as an undercover cop posing as a biker. *Sunset Beat* lasted only two weeks, but it left him free to take a part in *Baby Talk,* once again playing a construction worker.

This show, quite reminiscent of the *Look Who's Talking* movies, featured Tony Danza as the voice of baby Mickey. By now it was 1992, and Clooney's next show had a bit more longevity. He costarred as Ryan Walker, a homicide detective working under Lee Horsley's Lt. Ben Carroll in *Bodies of Evidence.* The next year he joined the cast of *Sisters* as another detective, James Falconer, who romanced Sela Ward's character, Teddy. They married at the end of the season and might have lived happily ever after, but in September 1994 Clooney started his rise to the top on *ER.* On the first *Sisters* episode of that season, Falconer was blown up by a car bomb.

2. **MARISKA HARGITAY**

Giving George Clooney a run for his money was Mariska Hargitay, who had regular roles in six series before sharing top billing in *Law & Order: Special Victims Unit.* Her TV series debut came in 1986 playing Jesse, a street-smart parolee living in a halfway house in *Downtown.* She next showed up as the cunning and scheming Carly Fixx on *Falcon Crest* in 1988. Series number three was 1992's *Tequila and Bonetti,* which tried to do the cop-and-slobbery-dog motif established in the 1989 Tom Hanks film *Turner and Hootch* one better by allowing the audience to hear the dog's thoughts.

Hargitay played the supporting role of Officer An-
gela Garcia. Another new series, *Can't Hurry
Love,* followed in 1995, and this time Hargitay was
Didi Edelstein, next-door neighbor to Annie
O'Donnell (Nancy McKeon) in this sitcom about a
group of friends in Manhattan that followed in the
wake of NBC's successful *Friends* series.

She next appeared in another cop drama,
Prince Street, as Detective Nina Echeverria, but
apparently NBC didn't quite know what to do with
the series. It aired on one Thursday in March 1997
with another episode appearing the next Wednesday, but then it was gone forever. Like Clooney,
Hargitay also put some time in on a top-rated
show, playing Cynthia Hooper, a somewhat flaky
girlfriend of Dr. Mark Green (Anthony Edwards) on
ER. In the fall of 1999, the days of short-lived series ended for Hargitay as she took a starring role
as yet another cop, Detective Olivia Benson on
Law & Order: Special Victims Unit.

3. HELEN HUNT

When Helen Hunt debuted in 1992 as Jamie Buchman in *Mad About You,* she seemed like a breath
of fresh air. A few viewers may even have recognized her as Murray's daughter from one episode
of *The Mary Tyler Moore Show* fifteen years earlier, but how many realized that *Mad About You*

was her sixth go-round on a TV series? As the daughter of renowned acting coach Gordon Hunt, it was only natural that she started acting at a young age. She wasn't yet a teenager when cast in her first series in 1974. *Amy Prentiss* starred Jessica Walter as San Francisco's chief of detectives—the first woman to have the job. Hunt played her daughter, Jill.

Hunt's next series a year later allowed her to taste a life of adventure as a shipwreck survivor on Irwin Allen's *Swiss Family Robinson*. Martin Milner played Karl Robinson, the head of the family, and Hunt played Helga Wagner, daughter of the lost ship's captain and the only non-Robinson to survive the shipwreck. Two years after that in 1977, she was back in the present day as next-door neighbor Kerry on *The Fitzpatricks,* a blue-collar family drama.

Legally an adult in 1982, Hunt was still playing a teen in her fourth series, *It Takes Two,* a sitcom with Richard Crenna and Patty Duke as a two-career couple trying to keep their home life together. Their daughter, Lisa, was played by Hunt; a young Anthony Edwards played her brother, Andy. Her last series stop before *Mad About You* was 1991's *My Life and Times,* an odd show set roughly forty years in the future. It featured elderly Ben Miller, played by Tom Irwin, reflecting on his memories, which took place a few years on either side of the present day, from a nursing home. Hunt played his wife, Rebecca, senile in her old age but vibrant in flashback.

4. CHRISTOPHER MELONI

Mariska Hargitay's costar on *Law & Order: Special Victims Unit* also traveled a long way through various series to get there. Christopher Meloni started in sitcoms but moved over to much darker drama. *The Fanelli Boys* was a 1990 sitcom about an Italian American widow whose adult sons moved back in before she could leave Brooklyn to retire in Florida. Meloni played not-too-bright Frankie Fanelli. His next sitcom had a similar title, *The Boys,* but it referred to older men. As writer Doug Kirkfield, he and his girlfriend relocated to help break his writer's block. They befriended their new neighbors, a group of senior citizens who absorbed Doug into their foursome. Doug didn't have long to worry about this, though, as the show only lasted a few episodes in 1993.

Another short-run series for Meloni was *Misery Loves Company,* which aired in 1995. As ladies' man Mitch DeMarco, Meloni lived with his recently divorced brother, Joe, who hung out with other, equally unhappy friends. This was hardly a laugh-a-minute premise, which may be part of the reason that only four episodes were broadcast. Meloni next had a go with the 1997 coroner's office drama *Leaving L.A,* costarring as investigator Reed Simms, but this offbeat series left the airwaves after only six episodes. It also starred Melina Kanakaredes, who later played Dr. Sidney Hansen on *Providence.*

While Meloni's series work was mostly comedic and light, his work in movies and guesting on other shows saw him as more of a tough guy. This image was notched way up when he joined the cast of HBO's gritty, uncompromising prison drama *Oz.* Unrepentant murderer Chris Keller was quite sexually active within the prison confines and gave Meloni an opportunity to explore the other side before taking the part of Detective Elliot Stabler, the sex crimes investigator he played on *Law & Order: Special Victims Unit.*

5. JENNIFER ANISTON

In 1994 another seemingly fresh face debuted in the form of Jennifer Aniston, who played Rachel on *Friends.* But by the time the Thursday hit debuted, she already had four series under her belt, the most out of *Friends'* cast of veterans. Her run of TV series came in a flurry, since she had only broken into television four years earlier in 1990. That first show was the teen comedy *Molloy.* Aniston played Courtney, Molloy's new stepsister and nemesis. The week after the final broadcast of *Molloy*, Aniston was back again, still playing a teen. She appeared as Ferris Bueller's sister, Jeannie, in the short-lived series based on the 1986 Matthew Broderick movie, *Ferris Bueller's Day Off*.

Aniston's next series, which followed in 1992, was a sketch comedy show called *The Edge*, in which she was part of the repertory cast, playing various parts in different episodes. In her final series before *Friends, Muddling Through*, she played Madeline, whose mother, Connie, had recently been released from jail. Connie had been doing time for shooting her husband, while Madeline kept the family truck stop open. That show ran only a few episodes, but Aniston didn't get much time off. The last broadcast of *Muddling Through* came just two weeks before the premiere of *Friends*.

6. JANE KACZMAREK

Just when it seemed like family sitcoms couldn't get more boring, along came *Malcolm in the Middle* in the year 2000 to make the form vital again. Malcolm's mother, Lois, the head of the Wilkerson household, may have looked somewhat familiar now that she was in her fifth series. Cable viewers were the first to see her series work in the early eighties when Showtime revived *The Paper Chase,* the law-school drama that had ended its run on CBS three years earlier. Kaczmarek played first-year law student Connie Lehman, the girlfriend of series star James Stephens's character James Hart. She jumped over to a network series in 1985 with *Hometown* on CBS. In the first episode her character, Mary Newell, married Ben Abbott, the man she'd been living with for the previous thirteen years. The show's obvious inspiration was *The Big Chill,* but it failed to share in that film's success. Next up was 1990's *Equal Justice,* about the Pittsburgh District Attorney's office. Kaczmarek appeared as Linda Bauer, who oversaw the DA's sex crimes unit. Sarah Jessica Parker was also featured in *Equal Justice,* which ran a season and a half.

Although Kaczmarek had been cast primarily in dramas, her career took a turn into comedy in 1993 with *Big Wave Dave's,* her last regular series before *Malcolm.* Here Kaczmarek played Karen Fisher, whose husband, Marshall, along with two of his friends, Dave and Richie, turned his back on the cold of Chicago to open a surf shop in Hawaii. The guys liked the soft lifestyle and left the details to no-nonsense Karen. As it turned out, that was good training for her role as Lois on *Malcolm in the Middle.*

7. **PATRICIA HEATON**

As Debra Barone on *Everybody Loves Raymond*, Patricia Heaton seemed to be a natural, but of course she had a few stops on her way to that role. She costarred with Linda Lavin in *Room for Two* during the 1992 season. Heaton was Jill Kurland, the producer of a daily talk show, *Wake Up, New York*. Her mother, recently widowed, moved from Ohio to live with Jill, and she quickly became a fixture as a commentator on the show. Heaton next showed up as the mother, Jean Stepjak, on *Someone Like Me,* a 1994 sitcom that focused on eleven-year-old Gaby (Gaby Hoffman). Jean, a somewhat strict, overly conscious neat freak, was often pitted against Dorie Schmidt, the much more relaxed and easygoing mother of Gaby's best friend, Jane. Unfortunately, *Someone Like Me* didn't get very many people like Gaby to watch, and it was canceled after only five episodes.

Heaton returned to playing an uptight single woman the next year in the *Designing Women* spin-off, *Woman of the House*. Delta Burke's *Designing Women* character, Suzanne Sugarbaker, returned as a member of Congress, finishing the term of her deceased fifth husband. The office was kept in order by Heaton's character, Chief of Staff Natalie Hollingsworth, but the entire affair was canceled, with only nine episodes airing. Four further episodes were later shown on Lifetime.

8. JENNIFER LOVE HEWITT

When Jennifer Love Hewitt joined the cast of *Party of Five*, she shook up a show that had already been getting quite a bit of attention for its performers. Before too long, however, Hewitt was receiving more attention than some of the original actors. But an overnight success always takes longer than twenty-four hours, and Hewitt had already seen three series come and go before she joined a hit. As she was only sixteen when she came aboard *Party of Five*, she had been busy for only a short time. Her first prime-time series, *Shaky Ground*, came in 1992. This sitcom starred Matt Frewer as a crazy dad, and Hewitt (credited here as simply Love Hewitt) was Bernadette, one of three kids. This show ran for about six months.

In 1994's *The Byrds of Paradise*, Hewitt again played the teenage daughter, here named Frannie. Timothy Busfield played Sam Byrd, a Yale professor who moved his family to Hawaii when his wife was killed. In this new environment Sam, Frannie, and her two brothers had to start a new life and come to grips with the death of their wife and mother. Seth Green played the oldest brother, Harry. Only twelve episodes were shown, so Hew-

itt was free when another series came along in the
fall of that same year. That series was *McKenna*,
an outdoors drama starring Chad Everett as
mountain guide Jack McKenna, the owner of Mc-
Kenna Wilderness Outfitters. Hewitt played his
daughter, Cassidy. This show also dealt with a recent loss, the accidental death of McKenna's son,
Guy. *McKenna* only survived for three episodes.
Party of Five portrayed the lives of the five Salinger
siblings (whose ages initially ranged from twenty-
four to one) after the deaths of their parents. This
became Hewitt's third series in a row to revolve
around coping with the loss of loved ones.

9. MEGAN MULLALLY

Megan Mullally won an Emmy in her second year
of playing cold-blooded, cocktail-swilling, unbe-
lievably rich Karen Walker on *Will & Grace*, which
was a firm affirmation that she had finally made it.
But, as is a familiar refrain by now, *Will & Grace*
was series number four for Mullally. Her first series
was 1986's *The Ellen Burstyn Show*, which
starred Burstyn as Ellen Brewer, a best-selling author living in Baltimore. Mullally played Ellen's divorced daughter, Molly Ross, who had moved
back to her mother's brownstone with her five-
year-old son. Also living with them was Ellen's
mother, Sydney, played by Elaine Stritch. Sched-

uled to immediately follow Lucille Ball's come-back series *Life with Lucy, The Ellen Burstyn Show* shared in Lucy's fate of a quick cancellation.

Mullally next appeared as a series regular on *My Life and Times,* the 1991 show that costarred Helen Hunt and told its present-day stories in the form of flashbacks from the year 2035. Mullally's contribution to the show took place entirely in the future. She played Susan, who worked at the retirement home and helped take care of Ben Miller. Her last appearance as a series regular before *Will & Grace* was in *Rachel Gunn, R.N.* This 1992 hospital sitcom starred Christine Ebersole in the title role. Although this show came and went quickly, it featured Mullally as Becky Jo, a character almost the exact opposite of Karen Walker. Becky Jo was a young, naive nurse whose problem was that she was too enthusiastic about her work.

10. COURTENEY COX, MATT LEBLANC, AND MATTHEW PERRY

Three of the *Friends* each had three series apiece to their credit before they became stars on that show. Courteney Cox was the most familiar face in the cast. Most prominently she appeared on *Family Ties* as Alex Keaton's girlfriend Lauren from 1987 to 1989. Before *Family Ties*, however, she was on 1985's *Misfits of Science* as Gloria, a reformed juvenile delinquent who fought crime with her power to move objects with her mind. Between *Family Ties* and *Friends,* Cox played Gabriella, the sister-in-law on *The Trouble with Larry,* a sitcom that aired only three times in 1993. Bronson Pinchot was Larry, who was honeymooning with Sally when he was lost in the jungle and presumed dead. Needless to say, his trouble was that he came back.

Matt LeBlanc had three shows behind him as well. In 1988's *TV 101,* he played a high school journalism student working on the school's cable news show. He played Vinnie Verducci, a prototype of his *Friends* character, Joey, on his next two series. Vinnie originally appeared on *Married . . . with Children* and was spun off into two different shows: *Top of the Heap* in 1991, which costarred Joseph Bologna as his father, Charlie, and *Vinnie and Bobby* in 1992, in which Vinnie had moved away from his father and lived with his friend Bobby.

Matthew Perry was another veteran of three shows before *Friends. Second Chances,* from 1987, started out as a fantasy sitcom in which Charles Russell (Kiel Martin), stuck in limbo between heaven and hell, was given a second chance to make his life better. He was returned to Earth to influence his teenage self, Chazz, played by Perry. In mid-season, the show was renamed *Boys Will Be Boys,* and Martin the semi-angel was out. Instead it focused only on Chazz and his friends. That wasn't enough to save it, but Perry was back in *Sydney* three years later, a sitcom in which Valerie Bertinelli played private detective Sydney Kells. Perry was her younger brother, Billy, a cop who would help Sydney out when she needed it. There was no home run here, either, so Perry was back again in 1993 with *Home Free,* where he portrayed Matt Bailey, a twenty-two-year-old still living a cushy life at home with his mother. That is, until his divorced sister moved back in with her two kids. That show lasted only four months, so Perry was willing and able when the producers of *Friends* came along.

21
It's Who You Know

During the nineties, one of the hottest acting jobs on TV was to appear as Jerry Seinfeld's girlfriend on *Seinfeld*. Jerry had trouble committing, of course, so the job was generally for only one episode—two at the most. The only ex-girlfriend who hung around for any length of time was Elaine. But because *Seinfeld* ruled the ratings during that decade, an appearance in just one episode resulted in very high visibility and could lead to big things. A number of *Seinfeld* girlfriends went on to their own regular TV series.

1. TERI HATCHER

Before she became Lois Lane in *Lois & Clark: The New Adventures of Superman,* Teri Hatcher raised her profile with an appearance as Sidra, Jerry's girlfriend with a big unanswered question: Were her breasts real, or had they been enhanced? Fortunately, Elaine was a member of Sidra's health club, so she went on an undercover assignment to find out. This being *Seinfeld,* of course, the subterfuge backfired and caused Jerry and Sidra to break up. Jerry did find out the answer he sought from Sidra herself: "By the way, they're real, and they're spectacular." In case Jerry didn't believe her, this was confirmed by lawyer Jackie Chiles (played by Phil Morris) in the final episode of the series. While waiting for the jury verdict that ultimately sent Jerry and the gang to prison, Chiles had the opportunity to spend some time with Sidra, who had testified against them. After the verdict was read, he echoed to Jerry: "They're real, and they're spectacular."

2. **JANE LEEVES**

Another high-profile girlfriend was Marla, the English closet organizer who also happened to be a virgin. Jane Leeves went on to appear in *Frasier* as Daphne Moon, Frasier Crane's father's physical therapist and Frasier's brother's initially unrequited, but finally requited, love interest for most of that series. Marla's status as a virgin became even more frustrating for Jerry in Leeves's second episode. He joined George, Elaine, and Kramer in a "contest," putting money down to see which one of the four could abstain the longest from certain "pleasurable activities." (Although the script never spelled it out, viewers knew they were talking about masturbation.) When Marla learned of the contest, she was revolted and walked out on Jerry immediately. By the end of the episode, however, she had lost her virginity as a result of meeting John F. Kennedy Jr. Marla also testified against Jerry and the others in the final episode's trial.

3. **COURTENEY COX**

The girlfriend getting the quickest starring part after an appearance on *Seinfeld* may well be Courteney Cox. She appeared as Meryl, a girlfriend who pretended to be married to Jerry in order to get a discount at the dry cleaners in March 1994 and debuted as Monica on *Friends* in September of that same year. Having already appeared as Bruce Springsteen's dance partner in his "Dancing in the Dark" video and as Alex Keaton's girlfriend on *Family Ties, Friends* was the show that rocketed her into the public's imagination. Although Jerry found the idea of pretending he was married to be intriguing in the beginning, he and Meryl quickly took on the worst aspects of married life, bickering endlessly with each other.

Photofest

Jerry Seinfeld may have suffered from girlfriend overload during his TV series, as a new girlfriend was introduced every week or two. Playing Jerry's romantic interest became a proving ground for actresses, many of whom went on to bigger and better parts in other shows.

4. DEBRA MESSING

Another actress who already had a TV show under her belt but was destined for much bigger things after her *Seinfeld* appearance was Debra Messing. She was starring in *Ned and Stacey* at the same time she guested on *Seinfeld,* but it was as Grace Adler on *Will & Grace* two years later that she received her highest profile. (In between, she starred in the short-lived science fiction series *Prey* as well.) As Beth on *Seinfeld,* she was in a crumbling marriage with David. Jerry and Elaine were each attracted to the wife and husband respectively and stepped in to console the separated couple, hoping to pick them each up on the rebound. Their hopes were dashed when husband and wife reconciled.

5. WENDIE MALICK

Wendie Malick was another actress who was recognizable from a number of appearances on various programs before showing up on *Seinfeld,* but she became much more successful afterward as Nina Van Horn, the spacey nymphomaniac fashion editor on *Just Shoot Me.* (She also starred in another brief show between *Seinfeld* and *Just Shoot Me: Good Company,* a sitcom about an advertising agency.) As the character Wendy, she introduced Jerry and his pals to the "kiss hello," which Jerry adopted to great success until he realized he didn't want to kiss every woman he met. Wendy also came under criticism from the gang for her "high school hair," a hairstyle that looked as though she had stepped right out of 1982.

6. PAULA MARSHALL

The actions of Paula Marshall's character, Sharon Leonard, resulted in one of the most oft-repeated lines from the series. Sharon was an NYU journalism student who was starting to date Jerry. She overheard a comment, however, that made her think she had a scoop. It all made sense: Jerry was single, he was in good shape, and he was very neat. She printed a story claiming that Jerry was gay. Marshall is the girlfriend who may have appeared in the most TV shows after her *Seinfeld* appearance: She has shown up on Fox's *Wild Oats,* NBC's *Chicago Sons* and *Cursed,* and ABC's *Cupid* and *Snoops,* and as the girlfriend of Michael J. Fox's *Spin City* character. None of these, unfortunately, led to long-term series success. (Not that there's anything wrong with that.) But Marshall was ready to try again in 2002 as Janine Barber in *Hidden Hills,* where she joined another former *Seinfeld* girlfriend, Kristin Bauer, who on *Seinfeld* had played Gillian, the woman with "man hands."

7. **KRISTIN DAVIS**

After her appearance on *Seinfeld,* Kristin Davis made the jump over to cable, becoming a regular on HBO's *Sex and the City* as Charlotte. She played Jerry's girlfriend Jenna, who, through no fault of her own, lost out on a longer relationship with Jerry. He accidentally knocked her toothbrush into the toilet and was repulsed when, unaware of that little detail, she continued to use it anyway. Try as he might, Jerry was not able to overlook his "toilet problem" with Jenna and had to break the relationship off. To Jerry's dismay, Jenna showed up on a later episode dating Kenny Bania, an unfunny stand-up comic who was something of a hanger-on to Jerry.

8. **A. J. LANGER**

With a couple of short-lived series, *Drexel's Class* and *My So-Called Life,* under her belt, A. J. Langer made a stopover on *Seinfeld.* After that *Seinfeld* appearance she went on to star in a couple more short-lived series, *Brooklyn South* and *It's Like, You Know,* and she landed the part of Annie on *Three Sisters,* which lasted over a year and thus became her longest-lived series. On *Seinfeld* Langer played Abby, a student in the field of risk management. Abby had adopted a mentor to guide her, a concept that intrigued Jerry. However, Abby's mentor was dating Jerry's hanger-on, Kenny Bania. Abby lost respect for her after she saw Bania's poor stand-up comedy act. In search of a new mentor, Abby focused on George, who was trying to prepare his own lecture on risk management.

9. KATHERINE LANASA

Another former *Seinfeld* girlfriend who found a home on *Three Sisters* was Katherine LaNasa. She went on to play the married sister, Bess. On *Seinfeld,* LaNasa portrayed Sergeant Cathy Tierney, a police officer. The topic of *Melrose Place* came up in her conversation with Jerry, who insisted he never watched the show. Cathy didn't believe him and challenged him to take a lie detector test. Of course, she was right. Jerry was lying—he was a big fan of *Melrose Place,* but he was embarrassed to admit it. Interestingly, the third sister from *Three Sisters,* Vicki Lewis, who played Nora, had also appeared on *Seinfeld,* but not as one of Jerry's girlfriends. She was once George's prim and proper secretary who displayed her wild side when she came on to him.

10. SUSAN WALTERS

If you don't remember the name of Susan Walters's character, don't worry—neither did Jerry.

He couldn't recall her name, and he couldn't find enough time alone with her purse to pull out her driver's license. He did learn that the name rhymed with a female body part. He and George suspected that it probably wasn't "Mulva." After several uncomfortable exchanges ("Oh, Jerry." "Oh . . . you."), the mystery woman realized that Jerry had no idea what her name was, so she walked out on him. Walters has since starred in two cable shows on the USA Network, as Anne Osborne on *The Big Easy* and as Lily Smith on *The War Next Door*. Her character's name on *Seinfeld,* by the way, was Dolores.

22

Where Have I Seen You Before?

To many actors, a job is a job—they're thankful to work in movies, on stage, or on TV (even if that sometimes means soap operas). They'll jump back and forth between the various media and the different styles of acting each demands. But once actors close in on the top of their profession, they see that acting has a definite hierarchy, and that movies definitely come in above TV. If they can successfully make the jump from TV to film (and not everyone can, as revealed by the careers of Shelly Long, Tom Selleck, and David Caruso), many never look back. Although soap operas have been a fertile ground for spawning movie stars, the following stars had regular roles in prime-time series before shifting over to the silver screen.

1. **WARREN BEATTY**

The classic example is Warren Beatty, who for a very brief time played spoiled rich kid Warren Armitage on *The Many Loves of Dobie Gillis*. During his run in the 1959 season, Beatty was on the small screen as Dobie's primary romantic rival, using his money to woo Thalia Menninger, the uninterested object of Dobie's affections. Thalia was played by Tuesday Weld, who also achieved considerable success in film. Although many stars who move from TV to film simply let their TV days fade away into the background, Beatty actively denied his for a time, claiming he had never worked in the medium. But those episodes of *Dobie Gillis* continue to live on, providing evidence to the contrary.

2. **LEONARDO DICAPRIO**

Movie stars don't get any hotter than Leonardo DiCaprio did after starring in *Titanic*. His film career, which had included *Romeo + Juliet, What's Eating Gilbert Grape,* and *This Boy's Life,* had been growing for some time, but he had a life before film. DiCaprio was a regular on two series in the early nineties. He played teenaged son Garry Buchman on *Parenthood* in 1990, a series adaptation of the 1989 Steve Martin movie of the same name, and Luke Brower, a homeless boy taken in to live with the Seavers during 1991–1992, the last season of *Growing Pains.*

3. MICHAEL KEATON

With different luck, Michael Keaton might have succeeded in a TV career rather than starring in movies. He was making his fifth series when he turned heads as Henry Winkler's partner in the film *Night Shift.* Each of his shows had been unsuccessful, some of them spectacularly so. In 1977 he played Lanny Wolf, an aide to President Jimmy Carter, in the political sitcom *All's Fair,* starring Richard Crenna and Bernadette Peters. He was a regular on both of Mary Tyler Moore's attempts at a variety show, *Mary* and *The Mary Tyler Moore Hour*; the latter featured him as producer Harry Sinclair.

Keaton and Jim Belushi starred as brothers Mike and Ernie O'Rourke, slapstick janitors in *Working Stiffs,* canceled after only four episodes. From 1979 until 1982 the performer had a fallow period, but he was in production on the sitcom *Return to Murphy,* in which he played a parole officer keeping tabs on his parolees, when *Night Shift* became a surprise hit. *Murphy* aired only a few episodes, leaving Keaton free to field movie offers.

4. STEVE McQUEEN

As bounty hunter Josh Randall in the Wild West, Steve McQueen starred on *Wanted: Dead or Alive* for three years, from 1958 until 1961. That's hardly an insignificant run, but his later career in such films as *The Great Escape, Bullitt,* and *The Thomas Crown Affair* was so stellar that it led many in the public to forget about the TV show entirely. McQueen appeared in *The Magnificent Seven* while he played Josh Randall, but it was clearly only a matter of time until the big screen demanded all his attention. Interestingly, in his final movie, *The Hunter,* he played Ralph "Papa" Thorson, a modern-day bounty hunter, bringing his career full circle.

5. **MICHELLE PFEIFFER**

Michelle Pfeiffer has two short-lived TV series to her name. But because she built her career slowly over a number of years, those appearances were several years before she received much recognition, and they've mostly stayed below the radar. The success of the John Belushi film *National Lampoon's Animal House* in 1978 inspired a raft of frat-house comedies on TV the next year, and *Delta House,* the official adaptation, lasted the longest, but still only a couple of months. Pfeiffer played The Bombshell, essentially window dressing. She missed out on another series when the part she auditioned for on *Charlie's Angels* was awarded to Shelley Hack later that year, but another chance appeared in the role of Samantha

"Sunshine" Jensen, an officer in a car-theft unit on Aaron Spelling's 1980 series *B.A.D. Cats*. She may have been just as happy when it lasted all of five episodes.

6.   JOHNNY DEPP

Although he reportedly had reservations about appearing in a role that looked like tailor-made teen-idol fodder, Johnny Depp agreed to star in *21 Jump Street*. After all, it was airing on the brand-new Fox Network, which at that time only aired programming on Saturday and Sunday nights. How successful could it be? After the show bombed, he likely hoped, he'd be able to get on with his career as a serious actor. As Officer Tom Hanson, part of an elite police unit that investigated crime in schools, he remained on *21 Jump Street* for its entire 1987–1990 network run, serving his time as a teen idol.

7.   CLINT EASTWOOD

Although Clint Eastwood is remembered as cattle driver Rowdy Yates on the TV series *Rawhide,* few people likely realize that he played that role for seven years, from 1959 to 1966. Eastwood experienced the TV actor's worst nightmare when he became so well known for his TV work that no film people would give him a job. He finally overcame that stigma by filming Westerns in Italy (they were called "spaghetti Westerns") during breaks in his *Rawhide* schedule. He made one each year in 1964, 1965, and 1966, and they brought him quite a following among European audiences. All three of those movies, *A Fistful of Dollars, For a Few Dollars More,* and *The Good, the Bad, and the Ugly,* were released in the United States in 1967 and finally, at the age of thirty-seven, a full-fledged movie star was born.

8. JENNIFER LOPEZ

It's become part of Jennifer Lopez's legend that she was a Fly Girl, part of the *In Living Color* dance troupe in the early nineties. But how many people are aware of the three other series in which she appeared? From December 1993 to September 1994, Lopez blitzed through one sitcom and two nighttime soaps. The first, *Second Chances,* was set in Santa Rita, California, and featured Jennifer Lopez as coed Melinda Lopez. *South Central* was a sitcom with a hint of drama, depicting a single mother raising her children in South Central L.A. Lopez played Lucille, a coworker at the co-op where the mother worked. In August 1994, Lopez had a second chance to play Melinda Lopez, this time on *Hotel Malibu,* another nighttime soap set on the California coast. By 1995, however, Lopez was on her way to film and musical stardom.

9. WESLEY SNIPES

A rising star in the late eighties, Wesley Snipes had appeared in a small part in Michael Jackson's "Bad" video and in a handful of movies. But in 1990, he likely hoped that he'd finally hit the big time when he starred in *H.E.L.P.*, a Saturday night crime show in which he played Officer Lou Barton. The initials stood for Harlem Eastside Lifesaving Program, in which Barton teamed with other police officers, firefighters, and paramedics under the direction of Chief Patrick Meacham. Meacham was played by John Mahoney, who later joined the cast of *Frasier* as Frasier's father, Martin, to much more success than he achieved here. *H.E.L.P.* lasted less than two months, but a year later Snipes finally found his star-making role in Spike Lee's movie *Jungle Fever*.

10. HALEY JOEL OSMENT

By the time Haley Joel Osment started seeing dead people in *The Sixth Sense,* he was already a seasoned showbiz pro with three TV series under his belt. At age six in 1994 he costarred with Ed Asner in *Thunder Alley,* playing Asner's grandson, Harry Turner. Two months after the last episode of that show was aired, Osment was back as Matt Foxworthy, a son on *The Jeff Foxworthy Show,* where he remained for two years. *Foxworthy* was canceled in May 1997, but the following September Osment joined the cast of *Murphy Brown* as her son, Avery, staying with the role until that show came to a close a year later when Osment was only ten. The year after that, 1999, was the year he became a household name.

23
Near Misses

When a TV show becomes a hit, the characters and the actors who play them are burned into our consciousness. We can't imagine how the show could have been any other way. Surely no one else could bring the same kind of life to these characters. But in many cases, someone else almost did.

1. GENE HACKMAN AS MIKE BRADY

When Sherwood Schwartz was creating *The Brady Bunch,* his first choice for the father was a young, up-and-coming actor by the name of Gene Hackman. At the time the show was being developed, Hackman had had a few parts in movies and TV shows, but he was far from a household name. The network executives had never heard of him, so they wouldn't even consider him for the part. *The*

Brady Bunch premiered in 1969 with Robert Reed in the role of Mike Brady. Two years later, Hackman made the film *The French Connection,* for which he won his first Academy Award. By the way, one of the names Schwartz considered for his show was *The Brady Brood.*

2. LLOYD BRIDGES AS CAPTAIN JAMES T. KIRK

Star Trek went through a lot of changes from Gene Roddenberry's original idea to the show that actually made it to the air in 1966. Most *Star Trek* fans know that a pilot with a considerably different cast was shot and turned down by NBC. Captain Christopher Pike, played by Jeffrey Hunter, helmed the *Enterprise* in that pilot. He evolved into James T. Kirk when the character and show were being reworked for NBC executives. At that time, science fiction was considered the stuff of B-movies, and Hunter, afraid the show might limit his career options, chose not to continue. The actor whom Roddenberry really wanted to lead his show, Lloyd Bridges, was also leery of appearing in a science fiction series and turned down the role.

3. THE COWSILLS AS THE PARTRIDGE FAMILY

In the mid-sixties, every kid wanted to be in a band. Four brothers from Rhode Island started a band, and soon their mother began to sing with them. Another brother and a sister later joined, making the band a real family affair (their father was the manager). The Cowsills started to get noticed, got a record contract, recorded some hits like "Indian Lake" and "Hair," got on TV, and became a big deal. Soon the offer came for the kids to star in their own TV show. But the offer was only for the kids—Shirley Jones had already been cast as the mother. The Cowsill kids didn't want to appear without their real mother, so they took a pass. The idea was still a good one, so the producers started auditions to find other actors for what became *The Partridge Family* in 1970.

4. BING CROSBY AS COLUMBO

The character of Lieutenant Columbo had been around for a while before Peter Falk came along. Created by Richard Levinson and William Link, Columbo made his first appearance in 1960 on *The Sunday Mystery Hour,* where he was played by Bert Freed. Levinson and Link next wrote a play featuring the character, *Prescription: Murder.* On stage Columbo was played by Thomas Mitchell, the character actor who had portrayed Uncle Billy in *It's a Wonderful Life* and Scarlett O'Hara's father in *Gone with the Wind.* Based on these performances, the creators envisioned Columbo as an older man, so when preparing a TV movie of *Prescription: Murder* in 1967, they ignored Falk when he lobbied for the role. Instead they pursued Bing Crosby, who reportedly turned them down because it would have interfered with his golf game. When Lee J. Cobb, their second choice, also turned them down, they half-heartedly let Falk have the part. Falk continued as Columbo, of course, when the character was given a TV series in 1971.

5. JOHNNY CARSON AS ROB PETRIE

Carl Reiner's first idea for what became *The Dick Van Dyke Show* in 1961 was called *Head of the Family*. Reiner played Rob Petrie (pronounced PEE-tree), head writer for *The Alan Sturdy Show*, who had a wife, Laura, and a son, Richie. That pilot was turned down by network executives, so Reiner retooled the show with the help of producer Sheldon Leonard, deciding to work behind the scenes rather than in the spotlight. One candidate for the newly available role of Rob Petrie (now pronounced PEH-tree) was a young comic named Johnny Carson, whose primary claim to fame was as host of the game show *Who Do You Trust?* He was ultimately passed over, obviously, for Dick Van Dyke, an actor Leonard saw on Broadway in the show *Bye Bye Birdie*. Carson did OK on his own. A year after *The Dick Van Dyke Show* premiered, he began what became an almost thirty-year stint as the host of *The Tonight Show.*

6. BRIDGET FONDA AS ALLY McBEAL

Producer David E. Kelley, a former lawyer, was getting ready to launch his third legal series. He had already won several Emmys for his work on *L.A. Law,* and *The Practice,* a show he had created that would go on to win several Emmys of its own, had debuted in March 1997. But for legal series number three, Kelley was interested in trying something a bit different. *Ally McBeal* would feature a young single lawyer whose fantasy and emotional life was dramatized on camera. He tried to get Bridget Fonda, who had never done a TV series, to take on the role, but she decided that she'd prefer to concentrate on a movie career. With no obvious second choice, Kelley started auditioning other actors and found Calista Flockhart, who rocketed to stardom in the role.

7. MICKEY ROONEY AS ARCHIE BUNKER

Like no TV show before, either drama or comedy, *All in the Family* challenged its audience's expectations and pushed the boundaries of what was acceptable on TV. Perhaps to put the audience at ease, producer Norman Lear sought a familiar face to head the cast and approached Mickey Rooney. Rooney thought that the character of Archie Bunker was un-American and, afraid that the role would harm his career, turned Lear down. The producer instead chose veteran character actor Carroll O'Connor, politically liberal himself, to take on the part. In a sidelight, the character of Archie's daughter, Gloria, was the last to be cast. Among the final choices for the character was Penny Marshall, girlfriend and future wife of Rob Reiner, who was already cast as Mike "Meathead" Stivic, Gloria's husband.

8. CARROLL O'CONNOR AS THE SKIPPER, JERRY VAN DYKE AS GILLIGAN, AND RAQUEL WELCH AS MARY ANN

Gilligan's Island was one show on which the casting was wide open. The hardest part to cast was the Skipper, and producer Sherwood Schwartz (yes, he also produced *The Brady Bunch*) saw a number of actors, including a pre-Archie Bunker Carroll O'Connor, before choosing Alan Hale Jr. His first choice for Gilligan was Jerry Van Dyke, but Van Dyke's agent wasn't impressed with the original script. Instead of *Gilligan's Island,* he booked Van Dyke in *My Mother the Car,* remembered as one of the worst shows in television history. After the first pilot, the actors playing Ginger, the Professor, and Mary Ann were recast. Raquel Welch auditioned to play Mary Ann, but the part, of course, went to Dawn Wells.

9. STEPHEN STILLS AS A MONKEE

The Monkees—Mickey Dolenz, Mike Nesmith, Davy Jones, and Peter Tork—were found through open auditions. That means hundreds of others also tried out for the group. One of those hopefuls was Stephen Stills, later of Buffalo Springfield and Crosby, Stills, Nash, and Young. The common wisdom is that Stills was turned down because he had bad teeth and hair. Stills has disputed this, pointing out that he could have fixed those things. He said he was passed over because he wouldn't give up the rights to any songs he might compose for the Monkees. Either way, everyone agreed that Stills was responsible for introducing the producers to Peter Tork, a friend and former bandmate. There is also an urban legend that aspiring musician and cult leader Charles Manson auditioned for the group. This cannot be true, however, as he was in prison at the time.

10. ROMA DOWNEY AS XENA

The producers of the syndicated *Hercules: The Legendary Journeys* found themselves in the mid-nineties with an unexpected hit. After several TV movies, *Hercules* became an hour-long series, and a spin-off featuring a female warrior was quickly planned. In the first film, *Hercules and the Amazon Women,* Roma Downey had played Amazon Queen Hippolyta and was the obvious choice for Xena. She negotiated for the role but decided to take the part of Monica on CBS's *Touched by an Angel* instead. Kim Delaney, who went on to *NYPD Blue, Philly,* and *CSI: Miami,* was also considered for Xena. A third actress, Vanessa Angel, was cast but had to drop out due to illness. The producers had to find someone quickly, so they chose unknown New Zealand actress Lucy Lawless, who had played one of Hippolyta's Amazon enforcers in the previous movie.

24
Success Breeds Success

Every year since 1949, the television industry (the National Academy of Television Arts and Sciences, to be exact) honors excellence in television programming and performance with the Emmy Awards. This is a very high-profile ceremony, and an Emmy award carries with it a tremendous amount of prestige. In most years particular TV series or performers tend to dominate the awards, but the identities of those dominators change from one year to another. From time to time, however, series and performers can maintain a high enough level of quality over a number of years that they take over their particular category and achieve a streak of Emmy awards. These are the longest streaks that have been maintained.

242

1. *FRASIER:* FIVE YEARS AS OUTSTANDING COMEDY SERIES

The longest streak of Emmy awards for a prime-time series is a relatively recent one. *Frasier* won the Outstanding Comedy Series Emmy for five straight years from 1994 until 1998. A spin-off of *Cheers, Frasier* brought Frasier Crane, the popular psychiatrist from that series, back to his home-town of Seattle, where he became a radio talk-show host helping callers with their psychological problems. He lived with his father, Martin, who had recently retired from the police force after being shot in the leg while breaking up a robbery. Also living with them was Martin's young physical ther-apist, Daphne. Frasier's brother, Niles, also a psy-chiatrist, lived nearby. *Frasier* became so well known for its preeminence in this category that in 2000, when Jim Carrey won his second consecu-tive Golden Globe Award for acting, his first re-sponse when he reached the podium to accept was, "Now I know what it's like to produce *Fra-sier.*"

2. *THE HUNTLEY-BRINKLEY REPORT:* FIVE YEARS AS OUTSTANDING NEWS REPORT

Although Walter Cronkite is fondly remembered for his years behind the anchor desk for CBS News, it was Chet Huntley and David Brinkley at

NBC who were winning the Emmys for Outstanding News Report from 1960 until 1964. Brinkley had been a journalist within the NBC structure for quite some time, but Huntley had come to work for NBC just the year before they were first brought together as a team. They anchored the 1956 presidential conventions together, where they made a strong impression. In fact, they made such a splash as a team that before the end of the year they had supplanted John Cameron Swayze's *Camel News Caravan* with their own evening news report. They coanchored *The Huntley-Brinkley Report* until 1970, when Chet Huntley retired to a ranch in Montana.

3. DINAH SHORE: FIVE YEARS IN VARIOUS CATEGORIES FOR BEST FEMALE PERFORMANCE

One idiosyncrasy of the Emmy Awards has been the way that categories have shifted around from year to year. This was somewhat understandable in the early years of the awards, as television itself was being refined and reinvented, sometimes on a daily basis. Singer Dinah Shore consistently won Emmys from 1955 to 1959, but she won them in four different categories. In 1955 and 1956, she won Emmys in the category of Best Female Singer for her fifteen-minute *Dinah Shore Show*. In 1956 and 1957 she continued the fifteen-minute program, but she also expanded to several hour-long specials. Since they were sponsored by Chevrolet, they were known as *The Dinah Shore Chevy Show*. She won in 1957 for Best Female Personality (Continuing Performance). *The Dinah Shore Chevy Show* specials became a full-fledged weekly series in the 1957–1958 season, and Shore's fifteen-minute program was phased out entirely.

Her 1958 Emmy came in the category that may have had the most convoluted name in Emmy history: Best Continuing Performance (Female) in a Series by a Comedienne, Singer, Hostess, Dancer, MC, Announcer, Narrator, Panelist, or Any Person Who Essentially Plays Herself. In 1959, the last year of Shore's Emmy-winning streak, the academy came up with a simpler name for the category: Best Performance by an Actress (Continuing Character) in a Musical or Variety Series. In addition to Shore's personal Emmys, *The Dinah Shore Chevy Show* won an Emmy in 1958 for Best Musical, Variety, Audience Participation, or Quiz Series and another in 1959 for Best Musical or Variety Series.

4. *LATE SHOW WITH DAVID LETTERMAN:* FIVE YEARS AS OUTSTANDING VARIETY, MUSIC, OR COMEDY SERIES

As of this writing, David Letterman's late-night comedy and talk show is in the midst of an Emmy-winning streak. From 1998 through 2002, it has won every year for Outstanding Variety, Music, or Comedy Series against such competition as *Saturday Night Live* and *The Tonight Show with Jay Leno*. If the show wins again in 2003, it will achieve the longest Emmy streak of all time. For almost thirty years in the sixties, seventies, and eighties, Johnny Carson ruled the late-night roost from his perch at NBC's *Tonight Show*. Although the other networks tried to program similar talk shows against him, Carson defeated all comers. During the eighties, Carson also produced a talk show to follow his own at 12:30 in the morning, *Late Night with David Letterman*. There was speculation that Carson was grooming Letterman to take over *The Tonight Show* after his retirement. Carson began to take more and more time off of his own show, and Jay Leno became a permanent substitute host when Carson wasn't there.

When Carson finally announced his retirement at the beginning of the nineties, many people, apparently including Carson and Letterman, expected Letterman to be named as his replacement. The leadership of NBC, however, chose to go another way, tapping Leno for the position. Across town, CBS, long thwarted in trying to mount effective competition to Carson's *Tonight Show,* made their own move, offering Letterman a considerable deal to come to their network. The executives at NBC offered to give Letterman *The Tonight Show* after all, but it was generally seen as a half-hearted gesture. In 1993 Letterman, reportedly with the blessing of Johnny Carson, made the jump from NBC to CBS. *Late Show with David Letterman* was immediately successful and took a quick lead over *The Tonight Show* in the ratings. This didn't last, however, and *The Tonight Show* ultimately regained its number one position among viewers. Letterman held onto his high standing among the critics though, as can be seen by his dominance in the Emmy Awards at the turn of the century.

5. *THE DICK VAN DYKE SHOW:* FOUR YEARS IN VARIOUS CATEGORIES FOR BEST COMEDY PROGRAM

When *Frasier* won its fifth Emmy in a row in 1998, it eclipsed the record that *The Dick Van Dyke Show* had set more than thirty years earlier. *The Dick Van Dyke Show* starred, as might be guessed, Dick Van Dyke as Rob Petrie, a comedy writer for a fictional TV variety program, *The Alan Brady Show*. It was based on the experiences of its creator, Carl Reiner, who himself had performed with Sid Caesar in *Your Show of Shows* and *Caesar's Hour* (he was also an unofficial writer).

Like Dinah Shore before it, *The Dick Van Dyke Show* won in the various shifting categories for which it was eligible between 1963 and 1966. In the first two of those years, it won in the fairly straightforward category of Outstanding Program Achievement in the Field of Comedy. The next year saw an odd experiment for the academy, in which it decided against separating out various categories and just made multiple nominations in a handful of catchall categories. *The Dick Van Dyke Show* was one of four honorees for Outstanding Program Achievements in Entertainment. (There had been sixteen nominees in the category.) Things returned to normal in 1966, when the show won in a category that made some sense, Outstanding Comedy Series.

6. *HILL STREET BLUES:* FOUR YEARS AS OUTSTANDING DRAMA SERIES

In many ways, *Hill Street Blues* turned television programming on its head. It featured a large ensemble cast of police officers from Hill Street Station, a station house in the ghetto of a large, unnamed city, and it gave reasonably equal time to each of them. This set the groundwork for other successful series to follow, such as *St. Elsewhere,* *L.A. Law,* and *ER.* Although it took awhile for the series to catch on with viewers, *Hill Street Blues* was an immediate hit with critics. It debuted in January 1981 and won its first Emmy for Outstanding Drama Series later that year.

In its first year at the Emmys, it set a record for the most Emmys won by a single series in a single year: eight. Dominating the acting awards for dramatic series that year, *Hill Street Blues* won Outstanding Lead Actor in a Drama Series for Daniel J. Travanti as Captain Frank Furillo, the commander of the station house; Outstanding Lead Actress in a Drama Series for Barbara Babcock as Grace Gardner, a police officer's widow who was having a passionate affair with a sergeant at the station; Outstanding Supporting Actor in a Drama Series for Michael Conrad as Sergeant Phil Esterhaus, Grace's sergeant and the leader of the daily roll call that opened each episode and ended in his trademarked warning: "Let's be careful out there." In other categories, the show won for Outstanding Writing in a Drama Series, Outstanding Directing in a Drama Series, Outstanding Cinematography for a Series, and Outstanding Achievement in Film Sound Editing. *Hill Street Blues* maintained its position as Outstanding Drama Series through 1984.

7. HELEN HUNT: FOUR YEARS AS OUTSTANDING LEAD ACTRESS IN A COMEDY SERIES

From 1996 until 1999, Helen Hunt took up residence in this category for her continued performance as Jamie Buchman on *Mad About You*. This series explored the marriage of a young yuppie couple, Jamie and Paul Buchman, who lived in New York City. Paul, played by series cocreator and coproducer Paul Reiser, was an aspiring documentary filmmaker, and Jamie was a public relations executive. The Buchmans had just been married as the series got underway, so the marriage grew along with the series. Helen Hunt received strong notices for the show from the very beginning, but it took a few years before the academy caught on. Hunt received three nominations before her first win.

It may have taken Candice Bergen, herself a multiple Emmy-winner for *Murphy Brown* (she won five in seven years for that show, but never more than two in a row, disqualifying her for this list), to finally put Hunt over the top. When Bergen won her final *Murphy Brown* Emmy, she expressed surprise that Hunt hadn't won instead. "Helen Hunt is my acting idol," were Bergen's words. The next year she took her name out of contention, clearing the way for Hunt. It's hard to tell whether or not this Emmy streak might have been able to continue. *Mad About You* left the air in 1999, the year Hunt won her final Emmy. In the midst of her streak of Emmy wins, Hunt also scored another impressive achievement: She won an Oscar for Best Actress in the 1997 film *As Good as It Gets*.

8. JOHN LARROQUETTE: FOUR YEARS AS OUTSTANDING SUPPORTING ACTOR IN A COMEDY SERIES

Although John Larroquette had already been acting for a number of years, he never received a great deal of notice until he was cast as Dan Fielding, the lascivious prosecuting attorney on *Night Court*. This series was almost the courtroom equivalent of the police house comedy *Barney Miller*. A collection of slightly odd regular characters led by Harry Anderson as Judge Harry Stone worked in the court, where the "night people"—those crazies arrested and brought into court in the middle of the night for who knows what—came to be tried, judged, and sentenced.

Larroquette has the distinction of winning every Emmy award for which he was nominated in this role. By 1989, however, he had had enough. After four consecutive wins, he asked that his name be withdrawn from consideration for any fur-

ther awards. Although he continued as Dan Fielding for the four remaining years that *Night Court*
was on the air, he didn't receive another nomination for the part. He has since been nominated for
Outstanding Lead Actor in a Comedy Series for his
own *The John Larroquette Show,* and he received
a fifth Emmy in 1998 as Outstanding Guest Actor
in a Drama Series for an appearance on *The Practice.*

9. *PLAYHOUSE 90:* FOUR YEARS IN VARIOUS CATEGORIES FOR BEST DRAMATIC PROGRAM

When people speak of the Golden Age of Television, programs such as *Playhouse 90* are what
they're talking about. Wildly ambitious, *Playhouse
90* set out to broadcast a new ninety-minute
drama, either an original or an adaptation of other
work, every week. What's more, during its first
year all the productions were broadcast live. Over
its four years on the air, 1956 to 1960, *Playhouse
90* produced such works as *Requiem for a Heavyweight, Days of Wine and Roses, The Miracle
Worker,* and *Judgment at Nuremberg.* Some of the
productions of *Playhouse 90,* including each of
these examples, were later adapted into feature
films.

The producers were able to attract actors such
as Paul Newman, Claude Rains, Errol Flynn, Maxi-

milian Schell, Ethel Barrymore, and Charlton Heston. The writers, such as Rod Serling, Abby Mann, and A. E. Hotchner, and the directors, such as John Frankenheimer, Arthur Penn, and George Roy Hill, were just starting out and went on to very successful careers in television and the movies. The Emmy awards *Playhouse 90* received during its four years included Best New Program Series, Best Single Program of the Year, Best Dramatic Anthology Series, Best Dramatic Series—One Hour or Longer, and Outstanding Program Achievement in the Field of Drama.

10. THE ACTRESSES OF *CAGNEY & LACEY:* SIX YEARS AS OUTSTANDING LEAD ACTRESS IN A DRAMA SERIES

Qualifying for this list with an asterisk, Tyne Daly and Sharon Gless, who played Mary Beth Lacey and Chris Cagney in *Cagney & Lacey,* tossed this award back and forth to each other for six solid years between 1983 and 1988. Daly received the award for the first three of those years, Gless won for the next two, and then it returned to Daly for the final year. Both actresses were nominated in each of the years that one or the other of them won.

Cagney & Lacey was a breakthrough show in the early eighties. Except for a couple of glamorous exceptions, such as Angie Dickinson in *Police Woman,* tough cops on TV were always male. This program suggested what might happen, for instance, if a cop team like Starsky and Hutch were women. In their personal lives, Mary Beth Lacey had a husband and kids at home, while Chris Cagney was single and looking for a relationship (as all single people on TV do).

25
Just Say Good Night

Television networks have often been identified by their news departments. Entertainment shows come and go, but the news has always been permanent. To a large degree, the public face of a network is its news anchor. In such a visible and significant job, it's important to make yourself memorable. Radio newscasters were often identified by their sign-off, the sentence or phrase that was the last thing they said on their newscast. This practice carried over into television and has produced some popular tag lines. One famous sign-off that doesn't qualify for this list is "Good night and good news." If it sounds familiar, that's because it's the phrase Ted Baxter used to close his newscasts on *The Mary Tyler Moore Show*.

1. JOHN CAMERON SWAYZE

One of the earliest TV news presenters (the term *anchorman* had not yet been used in this context), John Cameron Swayze rose to prominence very quickly. The technology was in its infancy, so Swayze was quite limited in what he could do. He couldn't do remote reports and he couldn't gather news footage, but he could sit behind his desk, introducing newsreels and reading the news. On NBC's *Camel News Caravan* in the 1940s and 1950s (sponsored by Camel cigarettes), that was pretty much what he did. At the end of every fifteen-minute newscast, he addressed his viewers and said, "Glad we could get together."

2. EDWARD R. MURROW

One of the few radio newsmen to make a smooth transition to TV, Edward R. Murrow became an American institution. In many ways, he set a standard for TV news that journalists still try to reach. In the 1950s Murrow hosted two different shows. The first was *See It Now,* a documentary series that provided in-depth coverage of the news of the day. At the same time, he hosted *Person to Person,* a more informal show that took a camera into the homes of celebrities who chatted long distance with Murrow back in the studio. First used on the radio when Murrow was reporting live from London during World War II, Murrow's famous sign-off was "Good night and good luck."

3. DAVE GARROWAY

Another television pioneer, Dave Garroway helped define morning news shows as the first host of *Today* on NBC. People didn't want hard news in the morning as they woke up and got ready for work, so Garroway, with his relaxed, comfortable manner, was just the ticket. Garroway was a friendly presence that was not too overwhelming in the mornings. And if anything did start to get too serious, there was always J. Fred Muggs, *Today*'s resident chimpanzee, to spice things up. When ending the show, Garroway raised an open palm to the camera and said one word: "Peace."

4. CHET HUNTLEY AND DAVID BRINKLEY

First working together anchoring the political conventions of 1956, Chet Huntley and David Brinkley made an impressive team. Replacing Swayze's *Camel News Caravan, The Huntley-Brinkley Report* ruled the TV news ratings for more than a decade. Every night they made their good-byes to close the show. "Good night, Chet. Good night, David." That closing was forced on them from above, and neither man liked it. Brinkley thought it seemed contrived—they talked to the viewers,

Chet Huntley and David Brinkley anchored NBC's evening news broadcast, *The Huntley-Brinkley Report,* from 1956 until Huntley's retirement in 1970. The partners were separated by distance, with Huntley broadcasting from New York and Brinkley from Washington. During the broadcast, they rarely addressed each other directly except to say good night.

not to each other. Huntley, who was originally from the rugged country in Montana, thought it made them sound like sissies. But the public liked it, and that's what counted.

5. WALTER CRONKITE

Walter Cronkite wasn't the first news anchorman for CBS, but he is by far the best remembered. His sign-off from the *CBS Evening News* was "And that's the way it is." Cronkite wasn't completely comfortable with that phrase. When he first started using it in 1962, he had envisioned closing the news each night with a human interest story. Depending on the mood of the story—amusing, thought-provoking, or even sad—he would respond with his line as a sort of comment on the report. When time limitations prevented the broadcast from taking this direction, Cronkite was still left with his sign-off, which he feared sounded too authoritative, as though he'd just told his audience everything they needed to know.

6.   HUGH DOWNS AND BARBARA WALTERS

For years at the end of *20/20,* Hugh Downs would say, "We're in touch, so you be in touch," and after he retired, the tradition was upheld by Barbara Walters. Although it's one of the most famous taglines in television, most people aren't sure quite what it means. Downs himself has been quoted as suggesting that the saying is a vague request for mail or other viewer response, as if he were saying, "We've just talked to you, now you talk to us." Whatever its exact meaning, it has proven over time to be a memorable phrase, and on TV that's far more important than actual content.

7. LINDA ELLERBEE/LLOYD DOBYNS

There was something about Linda Ellerbee's bearing that announced she didn't follow rules mindlessly. She never fit comfortably into the mainstream, but the work she did was always high quality. She cohosted two shows with Lloyd Dobyns. *Weekend* was a late-night weekend news magazine, and Ellerbee joined the program when it moved into prime time in 1978. The duo came back in 1982 with *NBC News Overnight,* which aired at 1:30 in the morning. Although Dobyns originated the sign-off, Ellerbee became more identified with it: "And so it goes." Dobyns claimed he borrowed the phrase from his parents, while others have suggested it came from the Kurt Vonnegut novel *Slaughterhouse Five.* Ellerbee, however, has pointed out that Vonnegut's phrase, "So it goes," is different.

8. DAN RATHER

Taking over the *CBS Evening News* from a retiring Walter Cronkite in 1981, Dan Rather tried various ways to put his own stamp on the broadcast. During one week in September 1986, he did that by experimenting with a different kind of sign-off. With no warning to his staff, on a Monday evening Rather signed off with one word: "Courage." His producers tried to talk him out of it, and critics and commentators just laughed. On Wednesday, following a story by reporter Bill Moyers about the U.S.-Mexico border, Rather closed with "*Coraje*," the word in Spanish. He abandoned the sign-off after the week and finally settled on the more restrained "And that's a part of our world."

9.   CHARLES OSGOOD

Newscaster Charles Osgood has moved back and forth between TV and radio, with a number of jobs on both. In 1994 he took over *CBS News Sunday Morning* from Charles Kuralt, who had hosted the program since 1980. It was a different sort of morning news show than *Today* or *Good Morning, America*. Like Sunday itself, this show was slower and more relaxed, taking its time to give its subjects the attention they deserved. At the same time, he anchored and wrote a daily radio news commentary, *The Osgood File*. Recognizing his dual role, Osgood signed off from *Sunday Morning* with the line, "See you on the radio."

10.   TIM RUSSERT

Meet the Press, TV's longest-running show, has had a number of moderators during its lifetime. In 1991 NBC News's Washington Bureau chief, Tim Russert, came on board to handle the show himself. Under his leadership, the program jumped to number one among the Sunday morning political news talk shows and displayed an impressive list of newsmakers who came in for an interview. Part of the reason for *Meet the Press*'s success as it finished its first half-century was Russert's almost nonstop promotion of the program in other NBC news programs. Even his sign-off was a promotional tool: "If it's Sunday, it's *Meet the Press.*"

Bibliography

Allman, Kevin. *TV Turkeys*. New York: Putnam Publishing Group, 1987.

Andrews, Bart, with Brad Dunning. *The Worst TV Shows Ever*. New York: E.P. Dutton, 1980.

Appelo, Tim. *Ally McBeal: The Official Guide*. New York: Harper Perennial, 1999.

Ball, Lucille. *Love, Lucy*. New York: G. P. Putnam's Sons, 1996.

Brady, Kathleen. *Lucille: The Life of Lucille Ball*. New York: Billboard Books, 2001.

Brinkley, David. *David Brinkley: A Memoir*. New York: Alfred A. Knopf, 1995.

Bronson, Fred. *The Billboard Book of Number One Hits,* Fourth Edition. New York: Billboard Books, 1997.

Brooks, Tim, and Earle Marsh. *The Complete Di-

rectory to Prime Time Network and Cable TV Shows 1946–Present. New York: Ballantine Books, 1999.

Brown, Les. *The New York Times Encyclopedia of Television*. New York: Times Books, 1977.

Carter, Bill. *The Late Shift: Letterman, Leno & the Network Battle for the Night*. New York: Hyperion, 1994.

Castelluccio, Frank, and Alvin Walker. *The Other Side of Ethel Mertz: The Life Story of Vivian Vance*. Manchester, Conn.: Knowledge, Ideas & Trends, Inc., 1998.

Claro, Christopher, and Julie Klam. *Comedy Central: The Essential Guide to Comedy*. New York: A Boulevard Book/published by arrangement with Byron Preiss Visual Publications, Inc., 1997.

Cronkite, Walter. *A Reporter's Life*. New York: Alfred A. Knopf, 1996.

Dawidziak, Mark. *The Columbo Phile: A Casebook*. New York: The Mysterious Press, 1989.

Denver, Bob. *Gilligan, Maynard & Me*. New York: Citadel Press, 1993.

Edelstein, Andrew J. *The Pop Sixties*. New York: World Almanac Publications, 1985.

Ellerbee, Linda. *"And So It Goes:" Adventures in Television*. New York: G.P. Putnam's Sons, 1986.

Essoe, Gabe. *The Book of TV Lists*. Westport, Conn.: Arlington House Publishers, 1981.

Fretts, Bruce. *The Entertainment Weekly Seinfeld Companion*. New York: Warner Books, 1993.

Gattuso, Greg. *The Seinfeld Universe*. Secaucus, N.J.: Citadell Press, 1996.

Graham, Jefferson. *Frasier*. New York: Pocket Books, 1996.

Green, Joey. *The Unofficial Gilligan's Island Handbook: A Castaway's Guide to the Longest-Running Shipwreck in Television History*. New York: Warner Books, 1988.

Harris, Jay S. *TV Guide, The First 25 Years*. New York: Triangle Publications, Inc., 1978.

Javna, John. *Cult TV*. New York: St. Martin's Press, 1985.

Javna, John, and Gordon Javna. *60s!* New York: St. Martin's Press, 1983.

Lewis, Jon E., and Penny Stempel. *Cult TV*. London: Pavilion Books Limited, 1993.

Marshall, Garry, and Lori Marshall. *Wake Me When It's Funny: How to Break Into Show Business and Stay There*. Holbrook, Mass.: Adams Publishing, 1995.

McCrohan, Donna. *Archie & Edith, Mike & Gloria*. New York: Workman Publishing, 1987.

———. *The Life & Times of Maxwell Smart*. New York: St. Martin's Press, 1988.

McNeil, Alex. *Total Television: A Comprehensive Guide to Programming from 1948 to the Present.* New York: Penguin Books, 1996.

Meyers, Ric. *Murder on the Air.* New York: The Mysterious Press, 1989.

Mitchell, Kathy. *Ally McBeal: The Totally Unauthorized Guide.* New York: Warner Books, 1998.

Moran, Elizabeth. *Bradymania! Everything You Always Wanted to Know about America's Favorite TV Family—and a Few Things You Probably Didn't.* Holbrook, Mass.: Bob Adams, Inc.

Owen, Rob. *Gen X TV: The Brady Bunch to Melrose Place.* Syracuse, N.Y.: Syracuse University Press, 1997.

Parish, James Robert. *The Hollywood Book of Death: The Bizarre, Often Sordid, Passings of More than 125 American Movie and TV Idols.* Chicago: Contemporary Books, 2002.

Pavese, Edith, and Judith Henry. *TV Mania: A Timeline of Television.* New York: Pavese & Henry Books, 1998.

Phillips, Louis, and Burnham Holmes. *The TV Almanac.* New York: Macmillan, 1994.

Schwartz, Sherwood. *Inside Gilligan's Island.* New York: St. Martin's Press, 1994.

Shatner, William, with Chris Kreski. *Star Trek Memories*. New York: HarperCollins, 1993.

Shepherd, Cybill, and Aimee Lee Ball. *Cybill Disobedience*. New York: HarperCollins, 2000.

Terrace, Vincent. *The Ultimate TV Trivia Book*. Winchester, Mass.: Faber and Faber, Inc., 1991.

Van Hise, James. *The Man Who Created Star Trek: Gene Roddenberry*. Las Vegas: Pioneer Books, 1992.

Waldron, Vince. *The Official Dick Van Dyke Show Book*. New York: Applause Theatre Books, 2001.

Weatherby, W. J. *Jackie Gleason: An Intimate Portrait of the Great One*. New York: Pharos Books, 1992.

Weisbrot, Robert. *Xena: Warrior Princess: The Official Guide to the Xenaverse*. New York: Main Street Books, 1998.

Whitburn, Joel. *The Billboard Book of Top 40 Hits, Sixth Edition*. New York: Billboard Books, 1996.

Wild, David. *Friends: The Official Companion*. New York: Main Street Books, 1995.

———. *Seinfeld: The Totally Unauthorized Tribute (Not That There's Anything Wrong with That)*. New York: Three Rivers Press, 1998.

Wiley, Mason, and Damien Bona. *Inside Oscar: The Unofficial History of the Academy Awards.* New York: Ballentine Books, 1986.

Williams, Barry, with Chris Kreski. *Growing Up Brady: I Was a Teenage Greg.* New York: Harper Perennial, 1992.

Index

About the Author

Douglas Tonks is a former editor for the *Hollywood Reporter*. He is the author of the book *Teaching Aids* and is currently a writer and book editor. He lives in Chicago.